The Good,

the Bad,

& the Yummy

The Good, the Bad, & the Yummy

FOOD THAT SUITS YOUR MOOD

By Adina Steiman

RUNNING PRESS
PHILADELPHIA • LONDON

9 8 7 6 5 4 3 2 1
Digit on the right indicates the number of this printing

Library of Congress Control Number: 2006931038
ISBN-13: 978-0-7624-2743-7
ISBN-10: 0-7624-2743-4

Cover and interior design by Amanda Richmond
Cover and interior art by Amy Saidens
Edited by Diana C. von Glahn
Typography: Metallophile, Coquette, and Sassoon

This book may be ordered by mail from the publisher.
Please include $2.50 for postage and handling.
But try your bookstore first!

Running Press Book Publishers
2300 Chestnut Street
Philadelphia, PA 19103-4371

Visit us on the web!
www.runningpresscooks.com

CONTENTS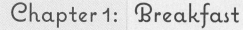

Chapter 1: Breakfast

good

bad

Chapter 2: Lunch

bad

good

ENERGY BREAK

NOONTIME LUXURY

Chapter 3: Dinner

Chapter 4: Mood Food

TEMPLE CALM

CARB COMFORT

Chapter 5: Party Time

SPA SOCIAL

SOUTHERN SOUL SHINDIG

Chapter 6: Share the Love

FANCY-PANTS TREATS

EASY-BAKE TREATS

Breakfast

It's a cliché to say that breakfast is the most important meal of the day, but even if you're technically fulfilling your breakfast-eating requirement, you might not be squeezing maximum benefit from the meal. If your boss needs to shout your name five or six times before you turn around and notice he or she is there, or if lunch seems incredibly tantalizing even though it's only 10:30 in the morning, you probably need a better breakfast.

Don't succumb to the stale muffins in the office kitchen! Beware the temptations of the deli around the corner! Instead, treat yourself to an honest-to-goodness, super-charged, healthy breakfast that will give you a big dose of energy. Start your day with self-affirmation ("I am good enough to deserve perfect granola") instead of self-destruction ("I don't care that I'm eating this donut") and you'll be smiling all morning.

¿

Go Good or Bad?
A QUICK DIAGNOSTIC QUIZ

if you

are sick of bad fast-food breakfasts, be Good

want to spoil yourself on the weekend, be Bad

think egg-white omelettes are for suckers, be Good

usually want to fall asleep at your desk at 10:30 a.m., be Good

want to get reacquainted with the joys of bacon, be Bad

?

good MORNING GLORY

There's something about a real breakfast, no matter how brief, that brings a serene focus to the morning. The rustle of cereal in a bowl. That first bracing sip of juice. The happy sound of an egg sizzling in a skillet. Even the simplest breakfast brings solace, helping you prepare for the day ahead, no matter how potentially gnarly it might be.

With only a bit of care, though, you can transform breakfast from special to spectacular. Greek yogurt, topped with a spoonful of honey and a layer of ripe fruit, beats the pants off the pre-sweetened commercial brands. Smoked salmon spread lasts all week in the fridge, ready to liven up your whole grain toast or crackers. Throw a handful of fresh chopped herbs into your scrambled eggs to add flavor and antioxidants. Swiss muesli is as nourishing as oatmeal, but twice as tasty.

Just like a bunch of never-fail outfits, these flavor-packed, nutrient-filled breakfasts will help you start your day feeling pampered and prized—all for less $$ than it costs to buy a double latte or a toasted bagel from the office cafeteria.

Greek Yogurt Parfait

In my humble opinion, this yogurt parfait is one of the premier accomplishments of the Greek civilization. This combination of a dollop of thick yogurt drizzled with a shining thread of honey and sprinkled with nuts and a generous helping of fruit is as healthy as an Olympic athlete—you get protein, dairy, fruit, and monounsaturated fats. Plus, it's so simple, you know it must be right.

Any fruit in season (i.e., cheaper and sweeter) works perfectly as a topping, from strawberries in spring and peaches in summer to pears in fall and grapefruits or oranges in winter. A few spoonfuls of the fruit compote on the next page is also a great option. Greek yogurt (look for the Total brand) is much thicker and more flavorful than regular yogurt, even in its low-fat incarnation, but you can always substitute with regular yogurt if necessary.

Makes 1 (10-ounce) serving

½ cup low-fat plain Greek yogurt

1 to 2 teaspoons fragrant honey

A few spoonfuls of granola or hearty
  breakfast cereal

Handful of walnuts or pistachios,
  roughly chopped

½ cup of your favorite seasonal fruit,
  chopped, or ½ cup Winter Fruit and
  Vanilla Compote (see page 14)

Place the yogurt in a small bowl or drinking glass. Drizzle with honey and stir until the honey streaks through the yogurt but is not thoroughly combined. Top with granola, walnuts, and fruit, stir, and dig in.

Winter Fruit and Vanilla Compote

Compote may seem like a food that only a grandma could love, but its soft texture and gentle flavor is the perfect complement to a bowl of yogurt, oatmeal, or muesli. Come winter, the compote treatment works especially well with hard fruits like apples and pears—with the help of a little sugar and spice, they become perfumed and tender. Dried fruits like apricots and figs also shine in compote, since the cooking revives them into juicy, chewy versions of themselves. This recipe is just a humble outline—feel free to substitute roughly equivalent amounts of whatever fresh and dried fruit you choose. Stash the compote in the fridge and it will keep for at least a week.

Makes 2 ½ cups

½ cup dried apricots

½ cup dried figs

1 apple, peeled, cored, and chopped

1 pear, peeled, cored, and chopped

½ cup light brown sugar, packed

A squeeze of lemon juice

1 teaspoon vanilla extract or 1 vanilla bean

In a medium bowl, combine the apricots and figs with 1 cup of boiling water and let the fruits plump up for an hour or so.

Place the plumped apricots and figs, along with their soaking liquid, in a medium saucepan along with the chopped apples, pears, brown sugar, and lemon juice. If you're using vanilla extract, add it to the fruit. Or, if you're using a vanilla bean, split it lengthwise and use a knife to scrape the seeds into the saucepan. Add the scraped vanilla pod.

Gently simmer the fruits over medium-low heat for 15 to 20 minutes, or until the fruits are soft but not mushy and the compote has reduced slightly. Let cool.

Smoked Salmon Spread with Lemon

In New York City, a bagel and a schmear is the quintessential breakfast. But while they're quick, cream cheese spreads are notorious for heading straight for the hips, and the bagel's no nutritional darling, either. Instead, try this savory, but still svelte, version on whole wheat crackers or toast. Feel free to top with sliced cucumber, tomato, and/or red onion.

Makes about 1 cup

¼ pound thinly sliced smoked salmon, roughly chopped

½ cup light cream cheese with chives, softened

¼ cup low-fat plain yogurt

1 tablespoon finely chopped fresh dill

Freshly ground black pepper to taste

½ teaspoon grated lemon peel

1 tablespoon freshly squeezed lemon juice

Combine all the ingredients in a food processor and pulse until smooth but still textured. Or chop the salmon finely and combine thoroughly with the other ingredients in a bowl. Adjust seasonings to taste.

Pan con Tomate

From bruschetta to panzanella, the Italians love to combine bread and tomatoes. But when it comes to breakfast, the Spaniards know best. In Catalonia, they rub toasted bread with garlic and tomato, and top it with a drizzle of olive oil. It's a perfect Mediterranean-style summer breakfast, especially since it gives you fiber, vitamins, and healthy fats. For extra protein, you can skip the olive oil and melt a bit of cheese over the top instead.

Makes 1 serving

2 slices crusty whole grain bread,
   lightly toasted
1 garlic clove, peeled
½ ripe tomato
1 teaspoon olive oil, 1 slice cheddar or
   Gruyère cheese, or 2 tablespoons
   fresh goat cheese
Kosher salt and freshly ground black
      pepper to taste

Rub the still-warm toast with the garlic clove. Squeeze the tomato so that it's nice and juicy, then rub the tomato over the toast, letting the pulp shred and pile up.

Drizzle the toast with olive oil, or top it with cheese and toast again just until the cheese melts. Season with salt and black pepper to taste.

Tri-Color Eggs

This is a great go-to egg dish when you need a quick infusion of energy and don't have the time to fuss with elaborate omelettes. Spinach and tomato cook up in a flash, and the crumbled cheese adds zing while being relatively low in fat. Pair this with a slice of whole wheat bread and a piece of fruit for a balanced breakfast that'll sustain you happily until lunch.

Makes 1 serving

1 whole egg plus 3 egg whites (or
   ¼ cup pre-packaged egg whites)
Kosher salt and freshly ground black
   pepper
1 teaspoon unsalted butter or extra-
   virgin olive oil
½ cup baby spinach (preferably the
   trimmed and pre-washed kind)
¼ cup chopped tomato
2 tablespoons fresh goat cheese or
   feta cheese

In a small bowl, whisk the egg and egg whites with salt and pepper. Set aside.

Heat the butter or olive oil in a small skillet over medium heat. Add the spinach and toss the leaves until they wilt. Add the chopped tomato and stir briefly.

Pour in the eggs and fold them into the vegetables until they are mostly set but still a bit runny. Sprinkle the cheese over the top of the eggs and gently fold it in, allowing it to melt.

Transfer the eggs onto a plate and eat while steaming hot.

Morning Platter

Sometimes, the best breakfasts are the ones you assemble instead of cook. Take the brilliant Continental breakfast. From Amsterdam to Jerusalem, people start their days with fresh vegetables, good bread, and whatever cheeses or salads they happen to have in the kitchen. It's a simple way to avoid breakfast boredom and undue effort—and it'll power you through your morning. Just stock some of the following items in your fridge, and mix and match during the week to create your own combinations. Take the time to track down German rye bread—it's dark, dense, and comes in blocks, and is packed with healthy seeds and grains. Swedish rye crisps are also terrific—they're usually much lower in fat and calories than regular whole-wheat crackers.

To ensure that you don't end up nibbling up a day's worth of calories, dish out your breakfast on a small plate before digging in.

Something Grainy

Whole-wheat or sprouted-wheat bread

Dense German rye bread with seeds

Swedish multi-grain crackers, like Wasa
bread or Ok-Mak

Something Substantial

Hard-boiled eggs

Fresh mozzarella cheese

Feta cheese

Fresh goat cheese

Swiss cheese

Something Fresh

Sliced cucumber

Sliced tomato

Zesty vegetable spreads like
muhammara, red pepper pesto,
Turkish salad, or Herbed and
Creamy Bean Spread, page 41

Marinated olives

Tender Strawberry Oat Bran Muffins

Muffins are justifiably popular for breakfast thanks to their portability and all-around deliciousness. Unfortunately, the American muffin has become the victim of super-sizing. Gargantuan muffins can clock in at over 500 calories. By shrinking muffins down to a svelte size and packing them with whole grains, fruit, and nuts, we can return them to the friendly breakfast companions they used to be. Of course, on weekday mornings, when you really need a muffin's portable energy and nutty taste, there's no time to bake! The solution? Rely on your freezer and toaster oven. Make up a big batch of muffins over the weekend, stash them in well-sealed freezer bags, and toss them in the oven at 350°F. for 15 minutes, or microwave them at the office for 2 to 3 minutes.

Makes 8 muffins

Nonstick cooking spray, optional

1¾ cups oat bran

¾ cup unbleached all-purpose flour

2 tablespoons granulated or light brown sugar

¾ teaspoon baking soda

2 teaspoons baking powder

1¼ teaspoons ground cinnamon

¼ teaspoon ground nutmeg

½ teaspoon kosher salt

1 cup fresh strawberries, roughly chopped

½ cup apple cider or orange juice

½ cup buttermilk

3 tablespoons good honey

3 large egg whites

2 tablespoons vegetable oil

1 teaspoon vanilla extract

Preheat the oven to 375°F. Spray eight muffin cups with nonstick spray or line them with paper liners.

In a large bowl, combine the oat bran, flour, sugar, baking soda, baking powder, cinnamon, nutmeg, and salt. Add the strawberries and toss well.

In a medium bowl, mix the cider, buttermilk, honey, egg whites, oil, and vanilla extract. Whisk this mixture into the dry ingredients until just combined. Divide the batter among the muffin cups.

Bake until the muffins are golden brown, and a toothpick inserted into the center of a muffin comes out with only a few crumbs attached, 25 to 30 minutes. Let cool for 10 minutes in the pan, then transfer the muffins to a rack to cool a few minutes more. Eat warm, or let cool completely and freeze in freezer bags.

Peach Quinoa Cereal

Do you love the idea of a hot, nourishing cereal, but get tired of plain-Jane oatmeal? Quinoa is the answer. It's a tiny, nutty-tasting grain that has a deliciously mild taste and crunchy-chewy texture when cooked into porridge—and it's a complete protein, making it much more nourishing than oats. Stir in some chopped peaches and spices, and it becomes an even more tempting breakfast option.

For maximum work-week efficiency, make up a batch on the weekend and divide it among reusable plastic containers. Keep them in the fridge, grab one in the morning, and reheat in the office microwave as needed.

Smoked Salmon Guide

Smoked salmon makes some of the best quick breakfasts. It adds nutritious luxury to a mostly egg-white omelette, a slice of whole grain toast, or a healthy spread (see the Smoked Salmon Spread with Lemon on page 15). But the varieties of salmon that are available can get as crowded as a Jewish deli on Sunday. Here's a quick guide to sorting through the variety, and some tips.

SMOKED SALMON is a generic term for just that—salmon that has been cold-smoked for flavor and shelf life. There are two main varieties: lox and nova.

LOX originally referred to salmon that was cured in a salt brine rather than smoked. Now it's generally cured and smoked, making it saltier than non-lox varieties.

NOVA originally described smoked salmon from Nova Scotia. Now it's a general term used to describe uncured, cold-smoked salmon, making it less salty than lox.

BELLY, when paired with *lox* or *nova*, describes smoked salmon made from the "belly" of the fish, which is generally fattier and juicier portion of the fish.

GRAVLAX is salmon that has been cured in a mixture of salt, sugar, alcohol, and spices—but not smoked. It generally has a juicier texture than smoked salmon, and lacks smoky flavor.

Homemade Herbal

If you already like herbal teas, you need no extra encouragement to drink them—you probably already know that they perk you up with their aromas without dosing you with excess caffeine. But you don't have to turn to a supermarket tea bag the next time you want a refreshing, steamy drink. Take a cue from elegant French ladies who are positively addicted to *tisanes*, the French version of herbal tea. If you think Red Zinger is cloying rather than refreshing, you'll enjoy the subtle refreshment of a tisane. Unlike American blends, tisanes are stripped down and simple—just a dried herb or two, steeped in hot water until its perfume and flavor is released. Pack up your favorite blend in a tin to preserve the aroma, or give some to a tea-loving friend who's getting tired of Earl Grey. Here are some directions for making your own, plus some classic tisane varieties—track them down at a health-food or spice store for the most aroma (and the lowest price).

To brew the tea, add ½ or 1 teaspoon of the tisane mixture to a tea diffuser, and immerse in a mug of hot water. Let steep for 3 to 6 minutes, depending on the brew and your taste. Sweeten with a bit of honey if you like, but skip the milk and sugar.

LIME FLOWER: Known in France as *tilleul*, this delicate, flowery tisane soaked Proust's madeleine in *Remembrance of Things Past*.

ORANGE PEEL AND CLOVE: Clove sweetens and spices the warmth of citrus in this tisane, which is great for winter. Make the dried orange yourself by drying the peel of two navel oranges in a 275°F. oven for 1½ hours. Blitz in the food processor until chopped, then combine with 2 teaspoons whole cloves.

LEMON BALM AND LEMONGRASS: A nice balance of herby and Asian lemon flavors. Combine ¼ cup dried lemon balm with ¼ cup chopped dried lemongrass.

PEPPERMINT AND VANILLA BEAN: This wintertime classic is both soothing and perky as a peppermint patty. Mix ½ cup dried peppermint with one chopped vanilla bean.

For the Love of Joe

IF YOU'RE A COFFEE LOVER, any coffee in the morning is good coffee. Great coffee, however, transcends mere self-caffeination. When you make it at home, careful attention to beans and brewing can yield a cup that beats the pants off most overpriced, underwhelming coffeehouse versions. Here's how.

The Beans: Fresh beans are paramount. Instead of dropping endless cash down the black hole of Starbucks, track down super-fresh roasted coffee from a local roaster. Unless you're truly obsessed with almond-mocha-flavored coffee, skip the flavored beans and head straight for the real thing. True coffee fiends claim that the tastiest coffee is roasted no more than a few days before it's bought—and should be used up in 2 to 3 weeks. Store it in an air-tight container in the refrigerator for maximum flavor retention.

The Equipment: Snag yourself a French Press and a coffee grinder if you don't have one already (they're available at any kitchen or gourmet store). A cone filter drip coffeemaker also works well.

The Process: Fill a kettle with cold water and set it to boil (or set up your coffeemaker) as soon as you've managed to stumble out of bed. Otherwise, you won't have time to brew and drink it before rushing out the door. Measure out about 2 tablespoons of whole coffee beans for each 8-ounce cup, and grind them until they resemble coarse cornmeal. Be careful not to over-grind your coffee—the process should only take a few seconds. Pour the beans, and then the boiling water into the French press and let the mixture sit for about 30 seconds. Press down on the plunger and enjoy.

A Sweet Toast

In the morning, jam on white toast can be too much of a sweet thing. It might be a lightning-fast breakfast, but the refined flour in the bread and the sugar in the jam usually lead to a major crash come mid-morning. What's the best solution for an a.m. sweet tooth? Just stick to fresh fruit, natural sweeteners, and whole grain bread—they digest more slowly and provide a steady source of energy.

Before layering on your fruit, top your toast with spreadable ingredients that have protein and fat, like fresh cheese or nut butters. You'll stay fuller longer, and their creaminess sets off fresh fruit in style. Here are some combinations to try:

- Crushed raspberries and honey
- Peach slices and almond butter
- Banana (mashed or sliced) and Nutella

- Sliced strawberries and pistachio butter
- Mashed banana, butter, and cinnamon
- Ricotta and honey

—bad←

DREAMY BRUNCH

The best weekend mornings can be summed up in one word—decadent. Tossing around in bed, surrounded by fluffy pillows and comforters, padding to the kitchen in soft slippers and an even softer robe, sipping coffee over the paper. The best part, of course, is indulging in some seriously evil brunch food. Big waffles, oozy omelettes, and crispy bacon are even more delicious for being illicit. I know plenty of folks who swear by brunch at their favorite restaurant, but there's one unforgivable drawback to that scenario—you have to get dressed, leave the house, wait ages for a table, and return home afterward in a calorie-induced daze. Hardly the right way to have a relaxed morning.

Instead, stick to your nest for brunch, and invite your friends over for a luxurious morning *a sua casa*. Complicated? Hardly. There's no need to offer every option on a typical brunch menu. Just pick one or two of these simple, rich, and super-easy recipes, and share a lazy Sunday.

Tangerine Mimosa

The mimosa is the quintessential brunch drink, and for good reason. Like the Bloody Mary, it cleverly masquerades as nutritious fruit juice but boasts a hefty dose of alcohol. While you can certainly use orange juice here, tangerine juice adds an especially luxurious note that's perfect for brunch. Real Champagne is traditionally used, but any good sparkling white wine works just as well. To make a Bellini, substitute pureed thawed peaches for the tangerine juice, and Prosecco for the Champagne.

Makes 4 to 6 servings

About a cup of freshly squeezed
   tangerine juice
1 bottle Champagne or sparkling
   white wine
Sprigs of fresh mint leaves

Pour about an inch of tangerine juice into each glass, then top up with Champagne. Garnish with mint, enjoy, and refill as needed.

Huevos Rancheros

At their simplest, huevos rancheros can be so very modest—just an egg topped with some salsa, maybe with a tortilla on the side. When they're dolled up with salty cheese, spicy black beans, and leafy cilantro, they become worthy of the centerpiece at brunch.

If you're entertaining, cook the eggs when everyone's at the table, and place a variety of bowls with all of the toppings on the table so your guests can add them to their eggs as they please. Then wait for the oohs and aahs.

Makes 4 servings

1 teaspoon vegetable oil,
  plus more as needed

½ cup finely chopped onion

½ teaspoon ground cumin

A pinch of dried oregano

2 (10-ounce) cans black beans,
  drained and rinsed

½ teaspoon kosher salt,
  plus more to taste

1 tablespoon chipotle hot sauce
  (Tabasco makes a good one)

4 medium-size corn tortillas

Your favorite salsa (roasted tomato or
  tomatillo salsas are especially nice),
  for garnish

Crumbled feta cheese or Mexican
  queso fresco, for garnish

Chopped fresh cilantro, for garnish

8 eggs

In a medium saucepan, combine the teaspoon of vegetable oil and onion over medium heat. Sauté the onion for 10 to 15 minutes, until golden-brown and aromatic. Add the cumin and oregano and stir constantly for 30 seconds to release the flavors. Add the beans, ½ cup of water, the salt, and hot sauce and stir together, mashing the beans a bit against the side of the pan. Reduce the heat to low and simmer, covered, for 15 minutes. Taste and adjust the seasoning, adding more salt and/or hot sauce if needed.

Meanwhile, prep your other ingredients. Set out the tortillas on a plate next to a small frying pan.

When the beans are ready, pour them into a tall bowl and bring them to the table with a small ladle. Set out the salsa, cheese, and cilantro in small bowls on the table.

Now it's time to warm the tortillas and cook the eggs. Heat the small frying pan over medium heat, place a tortilla in the pan, and heat for 30 seconds on each side, just until flexible and toasty. Remove to a plate and repeat with the remaining tortillas, covering the stack with a clean cloth as you go. Bring the tortillas to the table as well.

Add a bit of oil to the pan you heated the tortillas in, and cook two eggs for each person (I think they're best over-medium so they're still a bit runny in the middle). Bring the eggs to the table.

To assemble, take a tortilla, spread it with black beans, and place two eggs in the center. Spoon some salsa over the eggs, sprinkle with cheese, and shower in cilantro. The end result is as pretty as a Mexican flag.

Bringing Home the Bacon

Cream, butter, and eggs are all terrific components in a decadent breakfast, but every once in a while, only a few rashers of crispy, chewy, smoky bacon can hit the spot. Though all bacon varieties are dastardly, all bacon is not created equal. If you're going to indulge in porcine pleasure, be sure to get the most out of it by seeking out top-notch bacon.

- Generic supermarket bacon has artificial flavoring and is mostly fat, causing it to shrink down in the pan to a pool of foamy white grease. *Avoid it at all costs!*

- Center-cut bacon, often available at supermarkets, has more meat and is often naturally smoked over hardwood—it's also not quite as dastardly in its fat and cholesterol contents. *Try it out.*

- Bacon from the butcher is the best, usually thick-cut, meaty, and much fresher than the stuff from the store. *You'll fall in love.*

Buttery Eggs with Boursin, Scallions, and Shitakes

These eggs are pure luxury—tangy, savory, and luscious. Their rich taste is the essence of a luxurious weekend brunch. They're much classier than the average western or cheese-and-bacon omelette, and there's no need to worry about your omelette technique—simple stirring is the only thing these eggs will demand of you. Crispy things are the ideal accompaniment to these creamy eggs, so serve these with plenty of toast and crispy bacon.

Makes 4 servings

1 tablespoon unsalted butter

¼ pound shitake mushrooms, stemmed and thinly sliced

2 scallions, trimmed and thinly sliced

8 eggs

½ cup whole milk

1½ teaspoons kosher salt

¼ teaspoon freshly ground black pepper

1 package Boursin, or another garlic-and-herb cheese spread, crumbled

In a large skillet, melt the butter over medium heat and add the shitakes. Sauté, stirring occasionally, until the shitakes are tender and slightly golden. Add the scallions and cook for a minute more. Remove the pan from the heat.

In a medium bowl, whisk together the eggs, milk, salt, and pepper just until combined. Set aside.

Return the skillet with the shitakes to medium heat. When the shitakes start to sizzle, add the egg mixture and cook, folding with a spatula occasionally, until the eggs are almost done as you like them. Gently fold in the crumbled Boursin and cook for a minute or two more, until it melts.

The Good, the Bad & the Yummy

South Indian Coconut Eggs

Track down black mustard seeds and unsweetened grated coconut (both available at gourmet markets and health food stores), and you'll be equipped to whip up this spicy, exotic dish of eggs at a moment's notice. A dollop of plain yogurt will cool your tongue, and crisp toast, well-buttered, completes the picture.

Makes 4 servings

10 large eggs
1 teaspoon kosher salt
½ cup grated unsweetened coconut
1 teaspoon ground cumin
¼ teaspoon ground turmeric
¼ teaspoon ground cayenne pepper
2 tablespoons vegetable oil
1 teaspoon black mustard seeds
½ cup finely chopped onion
Cilantro leaves, for garnish (optional)

In a large bowl, whisk the eggs just until combined. Add the salt, coconut, cumin, turmeric, and cayenne and whisk well to combine. Set aside.

In a medium skillet, heat the oil over medium heat. Add the mustard seeds and cook until they pop, holding a lid over the skillet to prevent the mustard seeds from jumping all over the stove. Add the onion and sauté until softened and beginning to brown. Add the eggs, mixing until scrambled. Scrape the eggs into a large platter and top with cilantro.

Breakfast Sage Sausage

Before you flip past this recipe, I implore you to reconsider homemade sausage. It runs rings around store-bought versions, and takes next to no effort to make. No need to stuff it into sausage casings—just season some ground pork, shape it into patties, and fry. Sunny-side up eggs taste great alongside, or make pancakes and experience the taste sensation when maple syrup meets sausage.

Serves 4 to 6

1 pound ground pork

2 teaspoons minced fresh sage
  (or 1 teaspoon ground sage)

½ teaspoon kosher salt

½ teaspoon freshly ground black
  pepper

Combine all of the ingredients together in a medium bowl and stir well with a wooden spoon to combine the meat and spices. Shape the sausage meat into patties, big or small, and panfry over medium heat until well browned and cooked through.

Lazy Day Glamour

Whether you wake up on a weekday or a weekend, the same question looms—what to wear? Embrace the weekend and choose clothes that are the polar opposite of your practical weekday outfits. Slip into something as cozy and luxurious as brunch itself.

Think:

Your prettiest camisole or the perfect jersey undershirt
Silky boxer shorts, or comfy cotton pajama pants
Thick cashmere socks or sheepskin slippers on bare feet
Soft long-sleeved cardigan or the softest light robe

Buttermilk Raspberry Pancakes with Maple Crunch Butter

Let's face it—the blueberry is overexposed at breakfast. Not only is it the default berry in pancakes, it's even found its way into bagels! Raspberries give an extra dose of glamour that's complemented by sweet-and-nutty maple crunch butter in this recipe. And don't forget the bacon. As Agent Cooper remarked on Twin Peaks, "Nothing beats the taste sensation when maple syrup collides with bacon."

Makes 4 servings

FOR THE MAPLE CRUNCH BUTTER

1 tablespoon unsalted butter, melted

¾ cup sliced almonds

¼ cup granulated sugar

8 tablespoons (1 stick)
   unsalted butter, softened

½ cup pure maple syrup
   (ideally Grade B)

FOR THE PANCAKES

1 cup buttermilk

1 egg, at room temperature

1 teaspoon vanilla extract

3 tablespoons unsalted butter, melted

¾ cup unbleached all-purpose flour

½ teaspoon kosher salt

1 teaspoon baking soda

Unsalted butter as needed,
   for cooking

2 cups fresh raspberries

First, make the maple crunch butter. Preheat the oven to 375°F. In a small bowl, combine the melted butter, almonds, and sugar. Spread the almonds on a cookie sheet and bake for 10 to 15 minutes, until golden brown and slightly crispy. Remove from the pan to a plate to cool, then chop the almonds roughly.

In a medium bowl, beat the remaining butter until thoroughly softened. Gradually beat in the maple syrup, then fold in the roasted almonds. Set aside.

To make the pancakes, combine the buttermilk, egg, vanilla extract, and melted butter in a large mixing bowl until smooth. In a small bowl, whisk the flour, salt, and baking soda together until evenly combined. Stir the flour mixture into the buttermilk mixture just until evenly moistened.

Heat a nonstick skillet over medium heat. Butter the pan lightly, then ladle out about 3 tablespoons of batter per pancake, spreading the batter out a bit with the ladle. When the bubbles have just broken on the surface of the pancakes, nestle 4 to 5 raspberries into each pancake. Press the berries lightly with the spatula, then flip the pancakes and cook for about 30 seconds more. Repeat to make the remaining pancakes, and serve them topped with the maple crunch butter.

Giant Puffed Apple Pancake

Once you pull this apple-studded, yeasty treat from the oven, douse it in confectioners' sugar and rush it to the table, where you and one or two lucky companions can attack it with forks (or maybe even your hands).

Makes 4 servings

1 cup whole milk

4 large eggs

3 tablespoons granulated sugar,
    plus more for sprinkling

1 teaspoon vanilla extract

½ teaspoon kosher salt

¼ teaspoon ground nutmeg

⅔ cup all-purpose flour

4 tablespoons (½ stick)
    unsalted butter

2 Golden Delicious or Fuji apples,
    peeled, cored, and thinly sliced

Confectioners' sugar, for dusting

Preheat the oven to 425°F. In a large bowl, whisk until smooth the milk, eggs, sugar, vanilla, salt, and nutmeg. Add the flour and whisk just until combined. Set aside.

Place the butter in a 13 x 9-inch baking dish (preferably glass) and place the dish in the oven just until the butter melts, about 5 minutes. Remove the dish from the oven and spread the butter across the baking dish with a spatula. Arrange the apple slices neatly over the baking dish, return the dish to the oven, and bake for 10 minutes, until the apples begin to soften.

Pour the batter over the apples and top with an extra sprinkling of sugar. Bake for 20 minutes, or until the pancake is puffed and golden-brown. Dust with confectioners' sugar, cut into squares and serve warm.

Plum Crumb Cake

Bursting with purple fruit, big chunks of nuts, and plenty of cinnamon, these crumb cakes are pure heaven, and even more special since they release their divine perfume into your kitchen as they bake. The sight of plums sautéing in butter and sugar is sure to bring a blissful smile to your face. Slather a warm cake with fresh butter, and pair it with a terrific cup of coffee (see page 22) or black tea.

Makes one 13 x 9-inch cake

FOR THE PLUMS

1 tablespoon unsalted butter

8 to 10 small Italian plums, pitted
   and quartered but unpeeled

2 tablespoons granulated sugar

½ teaspoon ground cinnamon

FOR THE CRUMBLE TOPPING

¼ cup granulated sugar

3 tablespoons light brown sugar

½ teaspoon ground cinnamon

¾ cup unbleached all-purpose flour

¾ cup roughly chopped walnuts

5 tablespoons cold unsalted butter

FOR THE CAKE

½ pound (2 sticks) unsalted butter

2 cups granulated sugar

1 teaspoon vanilla extract

2 large eggs

1 cup sour cream

2 cups unbleached all-purpose flour

1 teaspoon baking powder

½ teaspoon kosher salt

Preheat the oven to 325°F. Lightly grease the bottom and sides of a 13 x 9-inch baking pan with butter.

For the plum filling, melt the butter in a large sauté pan over medium heat, then add the plums, sugar, and cinnamon. Sauté for 2 to 3 minutes, until the plums begin to soften. Set aside.

For the crumble topping, combine the granulated sugar, brown sugar, cinnamon, flour, and walnuts in a large bowl. Cut the butter into small chunks annd add to the bowl. Using your fingertips, work the butter into the mixture to make clumpy crumbs. Set aside at room temperature.

For the cake, cream the butter, sugar, and vanilla using an electric mixer on medium speed for 2 minutes, or until light and fluffy. Blend in the eggs one at a time, waiting until each is incorporated before adding the next. On low speed, mix in the sour cream for 30 seconds.

In a large bowl, whisk together the flour, baking powder, and salt; fold the flour mixture into the wet mixture just until incorporated.

Spread half of the batter evenly in the prepared baking pan, top with the plum filling, cover with the remaining batter, then sprinkle with the crumble mixture.

Bake for 50 to 60 minutes, or until a toothpick inserted in the center comes out clean. Move the pan to a wire rack to cool completely, then cut into neat squares to serve.

Music for a Luxurious Brunch

Like oil and water, some kinds of music just don't mix with brunch. Techno is too hard-edged and rhythmic; edgy pop or angsty indie music flattens the mood; and classical will put you right back to sleep. Here are some favorites that hit just the right brunch balance.

The Mamas and the Papas
18 Greatest Hits

Amazing harmonies and
the catchiest melodies.

Jelly Roll Morton,
Black Bottom Stomp

Old-time New Orleans jazz
from one of the masters.

Jonathan Richman,
*Jonathan Richman
and the Modern Lovers*

Simple, stripped-down pop songs
that will put a smile on your face.

Four Hawaiian Guys,
Greatest Hits

Nothing is more relaxing than music
straight from the balmy shores of Waikiki.

Caetano Valoso,
Caetano Valoso

Think "The Girl from Ipanema"—smooth,
soothing, sexy music from Brazil.

CHAPTER 2

Lunch

So you're busy as a bee at the office. Good for you. It's admirable to work

hard, even if you happen to spend half your time surfing the Internet. The stress of a

demanding job can lead to a depressing corollary—the routine of the dull lunch. Too often,

we stick with the same tired cafeteria salad or turkey sandwich from the deli, or we wile

away our hard-earned cash with expensive gourmet takeout or a hasty sit-down meal.

With a little effort, the lunch hour can be an oasis—one that can bring a dose of fresh-food

energy to the day or make you feel like a queen. Either way, you'll be the envy of even your

snobbiest colleagues.

¿

Go Good or Bad?
A QUICK DIAGNOSTIC QUIZ

if you

- have a pasty look to your face after a long day at work, be Good
- often wax nostalgic over the three-martini lunches of yesteryear, be Bad
- suspect that even the deli man is bored of your regular sandwich order, be Good
- want to stick to a healthy eating plan, but are tempted by fast food at noon, be Good
- wish you could swing a four-star lunch, but fear the wrath of your accountant, be Bad
- feel you're not getting your due at the office, be Bad

?

good ☞

ENERGY BREAK

Bravo. You've spent long hours sitting at your desk or sweating on a treadmill. If you don't pay attention, hunger creeps up before you know it, and unless you find a quick, smart way to satisfy it, you'll soon find yourself scarfing down French fries or ordering the usual dull turkey sandwich from the corner deli.

If you pack a wholesome, portable dish from your own kitchen, it's a whole other story. You'll restore your energy, keep your metabolism moving, and even help your muscles recover after exercise. The recipes in this chapter all stick to the three ground rules of healthy portable food: they're wholesome and tasty, with a good balance of protein, fat, and carbs; they keep at room temperature for a few hours; and they're simple to make and eat. It's all too easy for a snack from home to be as boring and bland as microwave oatmeal (especially if you're trying to make it healthy). Stick with these recipes, though, and you'll really be rewarding your virtuous, hard-working self.

A FEW TIPS:

Don't be afraid to cook in bulk. Making a week's worth of wraps or a batch of pumpkin-seed energy bars will eliminate the hair-pulling frustration of figuring out what to pack for lunch or a snack every single day.

Invest in good-quality plastic containers with lids. Buy the size that fit the lunch or snack servings that you prefer—avoid big, bulky containers that are annoying to pack!

Keep your cool. Even though this chapter's recipes can thrive outside the fridge, avoid leaving them in a hot car and don't be shy about stashing them in the office fridge if you can.

Mango Soy Lassi

Shakes are ideal for a quick lunch, or when you're prepping for or recovering from a workout. This mango treat is more nourishing than most, paired with yummy and beneficial bananas. Packed with potassium to prevent your muscles from cramping, plus plenty of iron and B vitamins, bananas are the perfect fruit for a midday snack.

Makes 2 (12-ounce) servings

½ cup vanilla soymilk

½ cup plain yogurt

1 banana

¾ cup chopped mango,
   fresh or frozen

2 teaspoons honey

Combine all the ingredients in a blender and puree until smooth and frothy.

Water, Water Everywhere

Experts recommend that people drink a stunning eight glasses of water a day. You might not think you need that much hydration when you're just sitting at a desk, but chances are if your energy drags in the afternoon, you need a tall glass of water rather than another cup of coffee or a greasy snack. Keep a bottle by your desk and you'll soon develop the habit of drinking from it all day. Reusing plastic bottles isn't the best idea, since chemicals from the plastic can leach into the water. So stop by a sports store and pick up a Nalgene bottle, which is made from a more durable plastic that's designed to be used over and over. If you get tired of plain water, squeeze a few drops of lemon juice into your water, or tote along a big bottle of one of the Spa Waters on page 115.

Very Veggie Sushi Rolls

Sushi doesn't have to be fussy. In fact, if you make it at home, you can skip the fish and pack it with vegetarian ingredients that will stand up to a few hours in your gym locker or bag. No need to slice it, either—you can eat it just like a burrito. Yes, these rolls are very veggie, what with the tofu and tempeh, but they also boast an addictive combination of creamy and crunchy textures that make them a true treat. Make up a few rolls and you'll have a feast-filled week.

You'll need a sushi mat to form the rolls—most supermarkets carry them in the ethnic food aisle, along with the rice vinegar and nori (seaweed) sheets. For maximum efficiency, start making the brown rice before you begin preparing the other ingredients. Once the rolls are assembled, wrap them tightly in two layers of plastic wrap to transport them easily. They'll keep for 3 to 4 days in the fridge.

Makes 4 sushi rolls

FOR THE ROLLS

1⅓ cups short-grain brown rice

¼ cup seasoned rice vinegar

2 teaspoons sugar

4 sheets toasted nori

FOR FILLING #1

6 to 8 ounces baked tofu, sliced into
   thin strips

2 medium carrots, peeled and cut into
   thin sticks

½ cup cashew halves, raw or roasted

1 avocado, pitted and diced

Cook the rice following the package directions until very tender. Meanwhile, prepare the ingredients for your choice of filling. Fill a small bowl with warm water and set aside. In a separate bowl, combine the rice vinegar and the sugar.

When the rice is finished cooking, transfer it to a large bowl and immediately toss it with the sweetened rice vinegar. Lay a sheet of nori, shiny side down, on the sushi mat. Dip your hands in the bowl of warm water, and use them to spread about ½ cup of the sushi rice over the nori, leaving a ¾-inch border along the top and bottom sides.

The Good, the Bad & the Yummy

FOR FILLING #2

1 (8-ounce) package tempeh,
   steamed for 10 minutes, then
   sliced into thin strips

12 shitake mushrooms, wiped
   clean and sliced

½ cup sauerkraut

1 avocado, pitted and diced

Layer one-fourth of the filling ingredients horizontally across the *bottom third* of the rice. Moisten the border on the top edge of the rice, then lift the bottom edge of the sushi mat (the edge that's closest to you) and use it to roll the sushi away from you as tightly as possible. When the sushi is fully rolled, use the mat to give it a final squeeze into the proper round shape. Repeat with the remaining three rolls, then wrap them in plastic wrap to store.

Herbed and Creamy Bean Spread

Beans are good for your heart! Lima beans, that is. And they're good for your energy level, too. This pastel-green spread, flecked with a bit of dill and lemon, is a nice change of pace from the traditional white-bean version. The blender does all the work, pureeing the beans into a snack packed with healthy carbs and fiber. Spread this on whole grain crackers, or use it as a dip for a bunch of baby carrots. To make a full meal, just pack a nice hunk of cheese alongside for some protein.

Makes 3 cups

2 (10-ounce) packages frozen
   lima beans (avoid baby limas)

2 tablespoons extra-virgin olive oil

1 garlic clove, minced

2 teaspoons chopped fresh dill

2 to 3 tablespoons lemon juice,
   or to taste

Kosher salt and freshly ground black
   pepper, to taste

Cook the lima beans according to package directions. Drain the beans and transfer them to the blender along with the olive oil, garlic, dill, and lemon juice. Puree until almost but not perfectly smooth. Season with salt and pepper.

Spinach Salad with Strawberries and Goat Cheese

A tangle of green leaves, creamy cheese, and strawberries, this simple salad is so good it should be bad.

Makes 2 servings

FOR THE DRESSING

1 teaspoon honey

1 teaspoon red wine vinegar

Kosher salt and freshly ground
   black pepper

2 tablespoons extra-virgin olive oil

FOR THE SALAD

4 cups baby spinach

½ cup sliced strawberries

½ cup fresh goat cheese

2 teaspoons sunflower seeds,
   lightly toasted

In a bowl large enough to hold all the spinach, whisk together the honey and red wine vinegar, along with a dash of salt and pepper. While quickly whisking, slowly pour in the olive oil and continue whisking until the dressing is smooth and almost creamy.

Toss the spinach with the dressing, and divide the leaves between two plates (if you're making this just for yourself, simply halve the recipe). Top each plate with half of the strawberries, goat cheese, and sunflower seeds.

Pear, Barley, and Gruyère Salad

This crunchy little salad is blissfully free of greens, so it waits quite cheerfully for you to eat it when you please. Gruyère, with its firm texture and nutty flavor, stands up well to the tart pear, and gives flavor to the chewy barley. The lemony dressing brings it all together. Because of the sustained energy you'll get from the cheese and the fiber-rich barley, this is an ideal pre- or post-workout snack or great lunch. You'll need to chill the barley for at least an hour after cooking it.

Makes 4 servings

FOR THE SALAD

1 cup hulled barley

2 pears, peeled, cored,
    and finely chopped

6 ounces Gruyère cheese,
    cut into small cubes

FOR THE DRESSING

Juice from about 1½ lemons

1 tablespoon chopped fresh mint,
    plus extra for garnish

Kosher salt and freshly ground
    black pepper

¼ cup extra-virgin olive oil

In a large pot, cook the barley in plenty of boiling salted water until tender, about 30 minutes. Drain the barley.

While the barley is cooking, make the dressing. In a bowl large enough to hold all of the cooked barley, whisk together the lemon juice, mint, and a dash of salt and pepper. While whisking, gradually add the olive oil. Continue whisking until the dressing is smooth and almost creamy.

Add the cooked and drained barley to the dressing and toss well. Chill for an hour or two, then toss with the pears and Gruyère. Taste and add more salt and pepper if necessary, and top with a bit of extra torn mint.

Drink Up

If you crave a drink that's cold and sweet in the afternoon, just dilute fruit juice with an equal amount of water or seltzer. You'll cut the calories in half and make the drink more refreshing to boot. Strong-flavored fruit juices are especially good when watered down—think black currant juice, orange juice, peach nectar, or mango nectar.

Szechuan Soba Noodles with Cucumber and Tomato

Sometimes, you're so starving by lunchtime that only carbs will do. There's no need to fall off the health wagon to get a dose of chewy satisfaction. Soba, or Japanese buckwheat noodles, are much better for you than regular white-flour noodles. They don't spike your blood sugar levels, and they're filled with Vitamins A and C. They also have enough backbone to stand up to a spicy peanut dressing like this one. Slivers of cucumber and tomato cut through the richness and cool the tongue.

Makes 4 servings

1 (8.8-ounce) package
   soba noodles

1 large seedless cucumber,
   peeled and cubed

1 small tomato, seeded and cubed

2 garlic cloves, peeled

1-inch chunk peeled fresh ginger

2 scallions, trimmed and roughly
   chopped

¼ cup chunky peanut butter

¼ cup tahini (sesame paste)

3 tablespoons soy sauce

First, prepare the noodles by cooking them according to package directions. Place the cucumber and tomato into a large bowl.

While the noodles are cooking, prepare the dressing. Combine the garlic, ginger, and scallion in a blender and pulse until you make an almost-smooth paste (add a bit of water if the mixture isn't blending easily). Add the remaining ingredients and puree until well blended.

Drain the cooked soba noodles, and add them to the cucumber and tomato. Top the noodles with the dressing and toss to blend. Eat right away, at room temperature, or straight out of the fridge.

The End of Salad Bar Chaos

The salad bar is the one part of the take-out lunch with which the home kitchen could never compete. How can you beat a huge variety of freshly cut vegetables, greens, fruits, toppings, and dressings? But the very thing that makes salad bars so attractive is also their undoing. So many options leads many people to create culinary chaos on their plates, piling a little bit of everything so that nothing tastes particularly good—or distinct. So here are some great salad bar combinations, all of which involve just six ingredients or fewer.

Cooked beets, shredded carrots, mixed greens, and a bit of avocado with wine vinaigrette

Mesclun greens, blue cheese, turkey, croutons, and sprouts with light Italian dressing

Romaine lettuce, hard-boiled eggs, cherry tomatoes, cucumber, sunflower seeds, and grilled chicken with light ranch dressing

Spinach leaves, grilled vegetables, goat cheese, and chickpeas with wine vinaigrette

Metabolism Boosters

Liquid calories usually have a bad reputation (think soda or sugar-packed fruit juices) but there are some important exceptions to the rule. These drinks and snacks boast rock-solid benefits for weight loss and health.

Grapefruit—Eating half a grapefruit or drinking a glass of grapefruit juice before each meal can help you lose weight. A Japanese study showed that people who consumed grapefruit three times a day lost an average of 3.6 pounds in 12 weeks—without making any other dietary changes. Pair grapefruit with a healthy lunch, and you could super-charge your metabolism.

Vegetable Juice—Drinking a glass or two of V8 or a similar vegetable juice before a lunch can trick your body into consuming fewer calories at the meal. Pick the low-sodium variety to avoid bloating, and spike it with some lemon or lime juice for extra tang and vitamins. Broth-based vegetable soups have a similar effect.

Chocolate Milk—If the last time you drank chocolate milk was at your best friend's fifth-grade birthday party, it's time to give it another go. People who drank low-fat chocolate milk after resistance training were shown to build twice as much lean muscle mass as those who drank carb- or electrolyte-based drinks.

Green Tea—Drinking plenty of green tea really does offer a host of benefits. Studies have shown that green tea can speed fat loss (especially visceral, or belly fat) and increase endurance during your workout. Drink 3 to 4 glasses a day (hot or cold) for optimal benefit.

Feel Good Inc.

Keeping up the pace at work can be as challenging (and exhausting) as sprinting on a treadmill. Late nights, impossible deadlines, and irrational bosses all sap strength and exhaust your energy. But there's no need to let the stress of work sabotage your plans to eat well. Instead, bring in the reinforcements. Keep a bowl of fruit on your desk for a quick snack. (Oranges are messy to eat, but their aroma is so uplifting!) Stash energy-boosting snacks in the office fridge, too—just combine carbs and protein into snacks like these, which offer long-lasting energy that won't weigh you down.

Apple slices and peanut butter

Hummus and baby carrots

Small bunch of grapes and a handful of nuts

Slices of tomato and fresh mozzarella

Sun-dried tomato spread on Triscuits

Yogurt and a banana

NOONTIME LUXURY

I've always envied the Italians. There are many reasons to do so, from their ability to stay svelte while consuming mountains of pasta to their mastery of gelato and killer leather pumps. But my biggest source of jealousy has been their old-fashioned habit of taking two or three hours off work for lunch. Many Italians still manage to go home, eat a meal with their families, and (this is the part that kills me) even take a short nap before returning to work. Italians know how to extract pleasure from life.

In America, we pride ourselves on being hard workers, not on pampering ourselves throughout the work week. But thankfully, most of us still do have that precious lunch hour. Why not take a cue from the Italians and extract maximum indulgence from it? Most of the day, you're beholden to someone else—at lunch, treat yourself like a queen. Leave your desk at noon and skip out for a 90-minute meal at your favorite restaurant. Even better, channel Molly Ringwald in *The Breakfast Club* and wow your co-workers with a ridiculously sinful and luxurious lunch you brought from home.

Oh-La-La Pâté Sandwiches

Most people think of pâté as an occasional luxury rather than a sandwich spread, but it's just perfect for sandwiches. The rich, earthy taste is addictive when layered on crusty baguette bread, especially when topped with a few pretty leaves of lettuce, some sliced ripe tomato, and thinly sliced cornichons (see below). Like peanut butter, pâté comes "chunky" or "smooth"—as a rough, country-style variety often called pâté maison or as a smooth mousse. Either variety will make you feel as elegant and discerning as Catherine Deneuve.

Makes 1 serving

1 five-inch piece of baguette

1 teaspoon unsalted butter, softened

Dijon mustard, to taste

3 to 4 tablespoons pâté

½ cup mixed greens

1 to 2 tomato slices

Split the baguette in half lengthwise, then spread each half with butter and Dijon mustard to taste. Spread the pâté on the bottom half of the baguette, then layer mixed greens and tomato slices on top. Press the two halves of the sandwich together firmly.

Smoked Salmon and Sour Cream Tea Sandwiches

Turn your lunch into a restful weekend brunch with these beautiful bite-size sandwiches. The caviar and fried onions are optional; both push this over the edge into big-time luxury. Any type of caviar will work here, from fancy Beluga to inexpensive salmon eggs.

Makes 1 serving

2 thick slices white or challah bread

2 tablespoons sour cream
  or crème fraîche

2 to 3 slices smoked salmon

1 teaspoon freshly chopped parsley

1 teaspoon store-bought French-fried
  onions (optional)

1 to 2 teaspoons caviar (optional)

Trim the crusts from the bread and toast them lightly. Spread sour cream on both slices, then layer with slices of smoked salmon and parsley. Sprinkle on the French-fried onions and top with a dollop of caviar.

Asparagus Frittata Sandwich with Truffle Oil

In tribute to those decadent Italians, here's a lunchtime classic from the land of the boot—frittata. An omelette is only good hot—a frittata is terrific hot, cold, or room temperature, making it a good choice for lunchtime. It's also much easier to make, since it's baked instead of rolled. Asparagus, that most elegant of vegetables, adds beauty and texture, and truffle oil adds that extra note of class. Thankfully, truffle oil isn't nearly as pricey as real truffles, and is easy to find at most gourmet shops.

Makes 4 servings

½ pound asparagus

2 tablespoons unsalted butter, divided

8 eggs

1½ teaspoons kosher salt

¼ teaspoon freshly ground
black pepper

½ cup grated Parmigiano-Reggiano
cheese

1 teaspoon white truffle oil

1 tablespoon extra-virgin olive oil,
plus more for brushing

4 ciabatta rolls, or other small
crusty rolls

1 cup mesclun greens

Trim the tough ends of the asparagus and cut into 1-inch lengths. Melt 1 tablespoon of the butter over medium heat in a large ovenproof skillet. Add the asparagus pieces and sauté for 5 to 8 minutes, until just tender. Transfer to a medium bowl to cool.

In another medium bowl, beat the eggs with the salt, pepper, and Parmigiano-Reggiano. Mix in the cooked asparagus and the truffle oil.

Preheat the broiler. Heat the large skillet over low heat, and add the remaining 1 tablespoon of butter and the olive oil. When the butter has melted, spread the oil-butter mixture evenly over the surface of the pan.

Pour in the eggs, and move the asparagus pieces around so that they are evenly distributed. Let the frittata cook on the stove for 8 to 10 minutes, without stirring, until the bottom of the frittata has turned golden and the surface of the frittata is soft but pretty solid. Transfer to the oven and broil for 3 to 5 minutes to lightly brown the top.

Invert the frittata onto a big plate, and let cool. Cut into rough squares and sandwich into ciabatta or other Italian rolls that have been brushed with olive oil and layered with some greens.

Green Goddess Sandwich

Just because a lunch is vegetarian doesn't mean it can't be luxe. Avocado, lime juice, pea sprouts, and wasabi mayonnaise make a dazzling combination of creamy, crunchy, and tart, with a little spice thrown in for good measure. Throw on some bacon if your inner carnivore gets the better of you.

Makes 1 serving

1 teaspoon wasabi paste or powder

3 tablespoons mayonnaise

2 slices French or Italian bread, toasted

½ ripe avocado

1 teaspoon lime juice

Pinch of cayenne pepper

Kosher salt, to taste

¼ cup baby arugula

2 to 3 slices bacon

In a small bowl, mix the wasabi paste or powder with the mayonnaise. Spread the mayonnaise on the bread, then layer with slices of avocado, sprinkle with a bit of lime juice, cayenne pepper, and salt, and pile on the arugula and bacon.

The Cheese Plate Lunch

When treating yourself like a queen at work, you must project an image of refinement and taste, as well. Nothing says indulgence *and* class like a cheese plate lunch. It's easy to schlep from the office to a picturesque park, simple to put together, and is a terrific way to discover new favorite cheeses. If you've stuck with the same Muenster, Swiss, or Brie for ages, it's time for you to expand your horizons.

In general, cheese plates work best when there are at least three types of cheeses: fresh, semisoft, and fully aged. Variety in the type of milk used is also a good idea—goat's milk cheeses generally have a nice tartness, sheep's milk cheeses are nuttier and gamier, and cow's milk cheeses are generally the richest, with rounded, full flavors. And don't forget the contrasting garnishes—the Spanish eat quince paste, the British have their chutneys, and Americans often keep it simple with dried fruit and a few nuts.

Italian Itinerary

- Fresh ricotta cheese
- Ripe, oozing Taleggio cheese
- Aged pecorino Toscano cheese

Pair with: dried figs, almonds, and crusty Italian bread

Très Français

- Aged goat cheese
- Semisoft cheese like Brie, Camembert, or Epoisses
- Firm, well-aged cheese like Comté, Cantal, or Beaufort

Pair with: a few niçoise olives, a fresh pear, and a crispy baguette

American-British Alliance

- Fresh American goat cheese
- Artisanal American blue cheese, such as Rogue River Blue or Point Reyes
- Super-sharp British farmhouse cheddar, like Keen's, Montgomery's, or Coolea

Pair with: mango chutney, pickled onions, and a few slices of a rustic oat loaf

GONE WITH THE WIND

One of the unsung glories of lunchtime at work is the opportunity to play hooky. Now that people take lunch anywhere from noon to 2 p.m. (and beyond), feel free to give yourself the royal treatment and disappear for more than your measly hour of lunch. After all, there's not much one can accomplish in an hour—you can't even count on going out to a restaurant and finishing up in 60 minutes! What if you want to multitask and go to the gym or hit a sample sale? There's no need to choose between essential lunchtime errands and lunch itself. Of course, not everyone agrees with this assessment, so here are some tips and tricks to make your lunch hour become lunch *hours*.

- Tell your boss you've scheduled a doctor's appointment around lunch. She can hardly blame you for being late returning. Feel free to add specific details if you want—"My bursitis is really bothering me, so I booked an appointment with my GP. . . ."

- Your desk should look like you've only been gone for a few minutes, so be sure to leave your computer screen on, and leave a purse or bag near your desk to imply you haven't left the building.

- Avoid long lunches with more than one colleague. It makes it way too obvious that the office has been abandoned.

- Depend on the responsibility of others. If you leave at noon and return at 2 p.m., the folks who only took an hour-long lunch will assume you did, too.

The Good, the Bad & the Yummy

Chocolate Luxe

From the time of the Aztecs, chocolate has always been a valuable commodity, a luxury item. Nowadays, chocolate has become positively glamorous. Modern chocolatiers are pairing chocolate with an unprecedented range of exotic flavors, from wasabi and ginger, to cardamom and rose. The flavors are so intense and unexpected that just two or three pieces of chocolate make a big impact.

What better way of concluding your ultra-luxe, shamelessly decadent lunchtime meal than with a few pieces of choice, highbrow chocolate? Warning: you will make your colleagues jealous, so pack only a few pieces at a time. Chocolate this good is meant to be hoarded, not shared.

Here are some of my favorite chocolatiers:

Fresh Herbs: Michael Recchiuti makes subtle, gorgeous chocolates in flavors like tarragon grapefruit, lemon verbena, pearl mint tea, and lavender vanilla (www.recchiuticonfections.com).

Asian Exotic: Jin Patisserie's Kristy Choo combines classic French chocolate-making technique with Asian flavors like pandan leaf, lychee, black sesame, and mango (www. jinpatisserie.com).

Spice is Right: Vosges Haute Chocolates goes way beyond vanilla and cinnamon. Exotic spices like fennel pollen, Hungarian paprika, Tellicherry peppercorn, star anise, guajillo chiles, and even curry add layers of flavor and nuance to these truffles (www. vosgeschocolate.com).

Tasty Textures: No one knows refined textures like a French chef. Jacques Torres makes an amazing assortment of chocolates with fillings that range from delicately crispy to gritty to unabashedly crunchy. Almondine and Butter Crunch, or Gossamer Wafer, anyone? (www. jacquestorres.com).

Champagne for Everyone

After-work office parties can be either boring or mortifying, but there's something nice about a little celebration during business hours. It's almost like a snow day or a fire drill—routines are broken and meetings cancelled—but you also get to pop open a bottle of Champagne. There's something deliciously naughty about knocking back a few glasses long before most happy hours even start. Even after the party's over, no one really gets back to work—people mill about, check their e-mail, and stare into space—in other words, they become deliciously careless. Here are a few excuses to throw the best kind of office party. Be sure to set up a pool for expenses!

clink!

Make a meticulous list of office birthdays and celebrate with cupcakes and Champagne!

Make going-away parties especially lavish so your departing colleague will remember you when she transfers to her new company! You never know when you might need a reference (or a spiffy new job).

Celebrate unexpected holidays like the winter solstice, Chinese New Year's, and Diwali. Check with co-workers and find out what unusual holidays they observe. No need to wait until Christmas!

Score points with co-workers and supervisors by hosting parties for projects accomplished, goals met, or super company successes.

CHAPTER 3:

Dinner

Sure, you can get dinner on the table in a flash. Order some take-out or zap a package in the microwave. But though you might be filling up your stomach, are you really satisfying your hunger? Dinner at home can be an end-of-day refuge rather than just another tiresome task—especially when you key your dinner to your mood. An exhausting day can leave you longing for the indulgence of a rich dinner, or the refreshment of a healthy one. Figure out what you need, then go forth and cook it.

¿

Go Good or Bad?

A QUICK DIAGNOSTIC QUIZ

if you

want to sever your ties with greasy takeout, be **Good**

deserve unabashedly rich satisfaction that's better than fast food, be **Bad**

can feel your favorite fancy skirt has gotten tighter, be **Good**

get the chills when thinking about steamed vegetables, be **Bad**

have dreams about sitting down to a dinner of whipped cream, be **Bad**

hate that your job is making you chubby, be **Good**

?

good

DR. FEELGOOD

A healthy meal always makes you feel better, but how about feeling your best? Pack your dinners with ingredients that brighten your mood, improve your alertness, and increase your energy—and you'll feel happy as well as svelte. An apple a day might not keep the doctor away, but the right "superfood" *can* cure what ails you. If you're feeling droopy after a long day of work, these recipes are the perfect antidote. If you're drained from a post-work workout, the buck stops here. If you want to slim down but actually like to eat, read on.

From a quick, citrus-packed salad to comforting soups, pan-seared fish, and an aromatic coconut curry, these recipes go far beyond mere nutritional obligation. With these recipes, what tastes great to you is actually great *for* you. So make your return from a long day into a chance for serious nurturing. Kick off your heels, get out of those fancy clothes, and turn on some music. It's amazing how your mind clears as soon as you smell the clean aroma of grapefruit or get distracted by the rich smell of cinnamon-scented chili.

Pink Grapefruit, Avocado, and Almond Salad

Grapefruits are good for you, of course—they're packed with vitamin C and bioflavonoids. In addition, cutting into a grapefruit is pure aromatherapy—with their steely sourness, they're even more refreshing and bracing than oranges. There are plenty more interesting ways to get your grapefruit fix than in the form of juice or the inevitable naked grapefruit half. I vote for pairing them with avocado. An equally healthy fruit, avocado adds luscious texture but remains resolutely healthy—with plenty of Omega-3 and Omega-6, vitamin A, and beneficial amino acids. The two fruits together yield a salad that perfectly blends tart and sweet, creamy and crunchy into a harmonious whole. And making yourself a pretty salad does wonders for your mood. If you love a beautiful salad, it's important to use ruby red grapefruits instead of the golden type, so that you get the lovely contrast between the deep pink of the citrus and the buttery yellow-green of the avocado.

Makes 4 servings

1 pink grapefruit

1 ripe Hass avocado

1 head romaine lettuce, torn into
  bite-size pieces

1 teaspoon extra-virgin olive oil

1 tablespoon red wine vinegar

Kosher salt and freshly ground pepper

A handful of slivered almonds

Cut the top and bottom of the grapefruit away to reveal the juicy flesh. Then cut the rest of the peel away from the grapefruit in wide slabs. Over a bowl, cut along the membranes that separate each grapefruit segment so that they fall into the bowl along with their juice.

Run a sharp knife lengthwise along the center of the avocado, cutting until you reach the pit. Twist the two halves away from each other, and scoop the pit out with a spoon. Using a large spoon, scoop out the avocado halves in one smooth motion. They should emerge in a lovely half-pear shape. Slice them into thin slices.

Arrange the lettuce in a wide serving bowl. With a painterly touch, arrange the grapefruit segments and slices of avocado on top. Drizzle with olive oil and vinegar, sprinkle on a bit of salt and pepper, and top off with almonds.

Curried Tofu with Cauliflower, Coconut, and Lime

An essential for your healthy-cooking arsenal, this saucy tofu dish packs in the vegetables and comes together in minutes. Coconut milk might sound like a dubious ingredient if you're trying to watch your weight, but studies suggest that compounds in the tropical fruit actually improve fat metabolism. Cauliflower and turmeric are both packed with antioxidants, and tofu provides filling protein to boot. This curry is flavorful enough to stand up to brown rice, though basmati will work, too.

Makes 4 servings

½ head cauliflower,
    cut into small florets

3 teaspoons canola oil

8 ounces extra-firm tofu, drained and
    cut into 1½-inch cubes

1 medium onion, finely chopped

1 medium carrot, peeled and thinly
    sliced on the diagonal

2 teaspoons curry powder

⅔ cup coconut milk

1 teaspoon kosher salt

A few grindings of freshly ground
    black pepper

1 lime

Heat a medium pot of lightly salted water to boiling, add the cauliflower florets, and cook them for just 2 to 3 minutes, until they're slightly tender but still crisp. Drain the cauliflower under cold running water, then set aside.

In a large skillet, heat one teaspoon of the oil over medium-high heat. Add the tofu cubes and use a wide spatula to lift and turn them occasionally, so a golden crust forms on almost all sides. Remove the tofu cubes to a small bowl and set aside.

Return the skillet to the heat and add the remaining 2 teaspoons of oil. When the oil is hot, add the onion and carrot and sauté until the onion becomes tender and begins to color. Add the curry powder and cook, stirring constantly, until the fragrance of the spices is released. Quickly add the coconut milk, along with the cauliflower, tofu, salt, and pepper, and stir well to combine.

Partially cover the pan and let the curry simmer for 4 to 5 minutes so the flavors combine. Remove the lid, add a squeeze of lime juice, and serve over rice.

Grilled Moroccan Chicken and Red Pepper Kebabs

A big bunch of leafy herbs is a delicious thing, especially when blitzed in the blender with garlic and toasted cumin to make a quick herby marinade for these chicken kebabs. Just toss chicken cubes in the mixture, and they're ready to cook in a grill pan or in the oven. What's more, the healthy protein of chicken breasts gets supercharged with the antioxidants and phytonutrients of cilantro, olive oil, and garlic. To make a full meal, heat up a can of mashed chickpeas with some fried onions and a dash of cumin and cinnamon. You'll need a package of bamboo skewers, available in the kitchen tool section of most supermarkets—be sure to soak them in water for at least 30 minutes before using them so they don't burn.

Makes 4 servings

2 teaspoons ground cumin

1 bunch cilantro

2 garlic cloves, peeled

2 tablespoons extra-virgin olive oil

1 teaspoon kosher salt

½ teaspoon freshly ground
   black pepper

3 chicken breast halves,
   cut into 2-inch chunks

2 red bell peppers,
   cut into 2-inch pieces

1 lemon

In a small skillet over medium-low heat, lightly toast the cumin, stirring constantly. As soon as it smells earthy and toasty, pour it into a small bowl to cool.

Grab the bunch of cilantro and pull the leafy part off, stems and all. You should have about a cup of leaves. Add them to a blender along with the toasted cumin, garlic, olive oil, salt, and pepper. Puree until you get a rough, emerald-green paste.

In a medium bowl, toss the chicken chunks with the cilantro paste. Thread the chicken onto skewers, alternating with the red pepper pieces.

If you're using a grill pan, heat it over medium heat and cook the kebabs, turning them a few times, until the chicken is golden-brown and cooked through, about 12 to 15 minutes. If you're broiling the kebabs, heat the broiler to 450°F. and broil the kebabs on a foil-lined baking sheet for 12 to 15 minutes, turning the kebabs at least once. Remove the kebabs from the heat, spritz with a squeeze of lemon, and eat alone or with a pile of chickpeas.

Turkey and Sweet Potato Chili

This chili is a miraculous thing. It's packed with ingredients that everyone knows are healthy—including antioxidant-rich tomatoes and black beans, disease-fighting chiles, and vitamin-packed sweet potatoes and peppers—but it tastes like full-on indulgence. Plus, it's made with ground turkey, which contains compounds that relax you after a tough day. I'm not a stickler for authenticity, but I think chili has to be gutsy. I want rich, spicy flavor from my chili—not a glorified vegetable stew. The solution couldn't be easier—canned chipotle chiles in adobo. Available in the Mexican section of most supermarkets, canned chipotles are just smoked and dried jalapeños, and they give a depth and bite to this super-quick recipe. Even though this makes a big batch of chili, resist the urge to halve the recipe—freeze the extra in individual portions and make your freezer happy.

Makes 8 servings

FOR THE TURKEY

1 pound ground turkey

½ cup finely chopped onion

2 garlic cloves, minced

2 canned chipotle chiles in adobo, seeded and chopped

2 tablespoons finely chopped cilantro

1 teaspoon kosher salt

FOR THE CHILI

2 tablespoons vegetable oil

2 cups chopped onion

2 garlic cloves, minced

2 green peppers, seeded and diced

1 red pepper, seeded and diced

1 sweet potato, peeled and diced

1½ tablespoons chili powder

1 teaspoon ground cumin

(ingredients continued)

In a large bowl, mix the turkey ingredients together with your hands until thoroughly combined. Set aside.

Heat a large pot over medium heat, and add the oil and onion. Sauté for 8 to 10 minutes, until the onions are softened and beginning to brown. Add the garlic, stir once or twice, then add the peppers and sweet potato. Sauté for a few minutes more.

Add the spices and stir constantly for 30 seconds to release the aroma. Add the meat mixture and stir, breaking up the meat and cooking until it's no longer pink, 8 to 10 minutes.

Add the salt, tomatoes, beans, corn, and cilantro, and simmer for 25 to 30 minutes, until the chili is thickened and the flavors are blended. Taste for seasonings, then serve with your choice of toppings.

¼ teaspoon dried oregano,
   crumbled

¼ teaspoon ground cinnamon

1½ teaspoons kosher salt

1 (28-ounce) can whole tomatoes,
   drained and chopped

2 (15-ounce) cans kidney beans,
   drained and rinsed

1 (15-ounce) can black beans

1 cup frozen corn

¼ cup chopped cilantro

TOPPINGS

Light sour cream

Chopped cilantro

Shredded cheese

Chopped scallions

Salty + Sweet = Quick Treat

If you're too busy to loiter long in the kitchen to make a light meal, don't bother turning on the stove at all. Stock your fridge and fruit bowl with good ingredients, and then it's only a matter of arranging them artfully on a plate, and voilà—lunch, dinner, or even breakfast. Here are some of my favorite combinations.

- Prosciutto, peaches, mint, and olive oil
- Fresh mozzarella, red ripe tomatoes, Spanish Serrano ham, and sea salt

- Roasted peppers, roast beef, ricotta cheese, and pesto
- Goat cheese, balsamic vinegar, wild arugula, strawberries, and black pepper

Seared Tuna with Cucumber-Cashew Salad

It's easy to feel intimidated by cooking fish at home. Even though it's one of the healthiest foods, with plenty of omega-3 fatty acids and protein, it cooks (and overcooks) very quickly. But if you know the big secret (it only takes a total of 2 to 3 minutes to cook), cooking tuna is as simple as can be. I like it raw in the center—the delicate taste works perfectly with the seared exterior. A simple soy syrup and a crunchy salad packed with cashews make this a purifying and satisfying dinner.

Makes 2 servings

FOR THE SAUCE

2 tablespoons brown sugar

¼ cup soy sauce

½ teaspoon grated lime peel

2 tablespoons freshly squeezed
   lime juice

A pinch of hot pepper flakes

FOR THE TUNA AND SALAD

2 (6-ounce) pieces ahi tuna

Kosher salt and freshly ground
   black pepper

½ English hothouse cucumber, peeled
   and thinly sliced

¼ cup cashews, roughly chopped

Squeeze of lime juice

1 tablespoon canola oil

In a small saucepan, combine all of the sauce ingredients and simmer gently over medium heat until reduced by half. Set the sauce aside.

Rub the tuna with salt and pepper. In a bowl, combine the cucumber and cashews and season them to taste with salt, pepper, and a squeeze of lime juice. Heat a medium skillet over high heat and add the oil to the pan, tilting the pan to coat it evenly. Add the tuna filets and cook, turning a few times, until the outside is lightly browned, about 2 to 3 minutes.

Remove the tuna from the heat and cut it into fat slices. Divide the tuna between two plates along with the cucumber salad, and drizzle the sauce over the tuna.

Crispy Salmon with Sweet Corn and Edamame

Nothing could be more simple than cooking up a piece of fish for dinner, and nothing else makes you feel quite as good. Sear a fillet of salmon skin-side down for a few minutes, pop it in the oven to finish, and enjoy the delicate taste and mood-boosting fish oils. Herbs add liveliness, and edamame packs plant estrogen. The colors are gorgeous, too—pink, yellow, and buttery green. If you don't have a large ovenproof nonstick skillet, transfer the seared fish to a lightly oiled baking sheet before roasting.

Makes 4 servings

FOR THE VEGETABLES

2 teaspoons unsalted butter

3 scallions, white part thinly sliced

1 teaspoon fresh thyme leaves
   (optional)

Kosher salt and freshly ground
   pepper, to taste

1½ cups fresh corn kernels
   (from about 2 ears)

1 cup frozen shelled edamame,
   thawed

FOR THE SALMON

4 salmon fillets, each
   5 to 6 ounces, skin on

Kosher salt

Scant ¼ teaspoon cayenne pepper

Melt the butter in a medium sauté pan over medium heat. Add the scallions, thyme, and a bit of salt and cook, stirring frequently, until softened. Add the corn and edamame and sauté for 3 to 5 minutes. Add more salt and pepper to taste. Cover the vegetables and remove from the heat.

Preheat the oven to 400°F. Place the salmon fillets skin-side up on a work surface, and pat dry with paper towels. With a sharp knife, make crisscross slashes through the skin (but not the flesh) of the fish. Sprinkle lightly with salt and cayenne pepper.

Heat a large nonstick ovenproof skillet over medium heat until very hot. Place the salmon fillets skin-side down in the pan and cook until the skin becomes crisp and brown, about 4 minutes. Flip the fillets over and place the pan in the oven. Roast the fish until it is opaque, about 6 minutes more.

Serve the salmon right away, with the corn and edamame mixture alongside.

Orange and Rhubarb Compote with Ricotta Cream

Sugary desserts usually lead to a nap-inducing dip in energy, but tart desserts wake you right up and boost your mood. The protein of ricotta cheese ensures sustained energy and, paired with citrus, makes for a terrific contrast of puckery tartness and creamy richness. You can make the rhubarb up to a week in advance and store it in the fridge. Throw the dessert together whenever you need a luxurious jolt of energy.

Makes 4 servings

⅓ cup sugar

½ vanilla bean

1 pound rhubarb stalks, trimmed
   and cut into 1-inch pieces

2 large navel oranges

2 cups ricotta cheese (fresh if possible)

⅓ cup confectioners' sugar

1½ teaspoons vanilla extract

In a medium saucepan, heat ½ cup water with the sugar over medium heat, stirring until the sugar is dissolved.

Split the vanilla bean in half lengthwise and scrape the seeds into the sugar mixture, then toss in the bean pod itself. Add the sliced rhubarb and simmer for 8 to 10 minutes, stirring occasionally, until the rhubarb pieces are tender but still holding together. Remove from the heat and let cool, then transfer to a bowl and chill in the fridge for at least 20 to 30 minutes.

When you're ready to eat dessert, cut the ends off the oranges and slice off the peel in slabs with a knife, revealing the orange flesh beneath. Slice the oranges into ½-inch-thick slices. Reserve the juices.

In a medium bowl, whisk the ricotta, confectioners' sugar, and vanilla extract together until blended and creamy. Whisk in the reserved orange juice.

To serve, layer orange slices, vanilla rhubarb, and ricotta cream however it suits your fancy.

Chocolate Angel Cakes with Blueberry Syrup

Light as a feather but intensely flavored, this cake boasts two antioxidant powerhouses: cocoa powder and blueberries. Use a great cocoa powder like Scharffen-Berger or Valrhona for deeper flavor.

Makes 1 (10-inch) cake

FOR THE CAKE

¼ cup plus 2 tablespoons
  unsweetened cocoa powder

¼ teaspoon ground nutmeg

¼ cup boiling water

2 teaspoons pure vanilla extract

1 cup sifted cake flour

1¾ cups sugar

¼ teaspoon kosher salt

16 large egg whites

2 teaspoons cream of tartar

FOR THE BLUEBERRY SYRUP

2 cups blueberries

½ cup sugar

1 teaspoon vanilla extract

Preheat the oven to 350°F. In a large bowl, whisk together the cocoa and nutmeg, then gradually whisk in the boiling water and then the vanilla extract. Cover and set aside.

In a medium bowl, whisk together the cake flour, ¾ cup of sugar, and the salt. Set aside.

In a large, clean bowl, using clean beaters, whip the egg whites with an electric mixer just until frothy. Add the cream of tartar, then continue beating until soft peaks form. Continue beating as you gradually add the remaining 1 cup of sugar, then beat until stiff peaks form.

Using a rubber spatula, gently fold in the flour mixture, ¼ cup at a time. Whisk 1 cup of the egg white mixture into the cocoa mixture, then transfer the remaining egg white mixture to the cocoa-mixture bowl and fold them together until almost completely combined.

Pour the batter into an ungreased 10-inch tube pan, run a knife through the batter to eliminate air pockets, and bake for 50 minutes, or until a knife inserted in the center comes out clean. Invert over a wine bottle and let cool completely. Run a thin knife around the edge of the pan and the tube to loosen the cake, then invert onto a serving plate.

Meanwhile, combine the blueberries, sugar, vanilla extract, and ¼ cup of water, and simmer until most of the berries pop and the syrup has thickened. Top each slice of cake with a generous dose of the warm blueberry syrup.

Wine Rx

PACKED WITH ANTIOXIDANTS, a glass or two of wine is a healthy way to wind down after a long day at work. If you find yourself always making a beeline for the Chardonnay or Merlot at the wine store, chances are you're missing out on even more interesting (and probably cheaper) wines from beyond our borders. But how to go about conquering the wide world of wines? Take a cue from the American varietals you already know you like, and try out a wine with a similar flavor profile.

IF YOU LIKE:	Champagne	Chardonnay	Merlot	Pinot Noir	Cabernet
CHECK OUT:	Prosecco	Gewürztraminer	Valpolicella	Chianti	Amarone

Don't Fear the Olive

Ever since the advent of the low-fat diet, we've been taught to request fat-free dressings for our salads and avoid butter on our vegetables. But research shows that your body actually needs some fat to absorb the nutrients in vegetables. Pick heart-healthy natural fats like olive oil and organic butter, and avoid engineered replacements like margarine.

—bad⇄

SHAMELESS INSTANT DINNER

No more Cup-O-Noodles and ramen soup! Away with frozen dinners and overpriced takeout! Late nights at work might make us ravenous and too tired to whip up a soufflé, but that doesn't mean we have to eat unsatisfying food. On the contrary. We need a big dose of lusciousness to soothe our souls at the end of a long day.

That's where this crop of recipes comes into play. They use shortcut ingredients like frozen tater tots and canned tuna, they don't demand much time or effort, and they taste like real dinner. They even work when you're impatient and hungry.

Chipotle Meatballs with Cilantro

This dish is an unlikely flirtation between Italian and Mexican classics, but it works. Mexican chipotle chiles add spiciness and a rich smoky flavor to a simple tomato sauce. If you add store-bought meatballs and simmer them for a half hour, you get an über-rich dish that runs rings around bottled marinara. Canned chipotle chiles are usually pretty easy to find in the Mexican section of the ethnic food aisle at most supermarkets. Serve with plenty of crusty bread and a fat mango for dessert.

Makes 3 to 4 servings

1 tablespoon vegetable oil

2 garlic cloves, peeled
   and thinly sliced

1 teaspoon ground cumin

¼ teaspoon dried oregano

1 (28-ounce) can whole Italian
   tomatoes, drained

1¼ teaspoon kosher salt

2 to 3 canned chipotle chiles in adobo,
   seeded and finely chopped

1 pound store-bought regular or mini
   meatballs, thawed if frozen

¼ cup roughly chopped cilantro

Heat the oil in a medium saucepan over medium heat. Add the garlic and cook just until golden, then quickly stir in the cumin and oregano and cook for just a few seconds. Add the tomatoes, salt, and chipotles, and crush the tomatoes with a spatula. Bring the sauce to a simmer and cook for 10 minutes. Add the meatballs and cook for 15 to 20 minutes more, until the sauce is reduced. Top with cilantro before devouring.

Ravioli with Black Olive and Tomato Butter

What's so special about ricotta ravioli? On its own, nothing much, but when you grab a package from the refrigerated section of the supermarket and add olive-and-tomato flecked butter, it's transformed. Always keep a tube of black olive paste in your fridge—it's great on crostini or toast as a snack. You can find it in gourmet shops and the Italian section of supermarkets.

Makes 2 servings

1 (16-ounce) package ricotta
or three-cheese ravioli

2 tablespoons unsalted butter

1 garlic clove, minced

1 tablespoon black olive paste

4 plum tomatoes, seeded and finely
chopped

4 basil leaves, roughly torn

Parmesan cheese, for serving
(optional)

Cook the ravioli according to package directions.

While the ravioli is cooking, melt the butter in a medium skillet. Add the garlic and sauté until light gold. Immediately stir in the black olive paste and then the tomatoes. Cook until the tomatoes give up a bit of their juice and the mixture looks saucy. Add the basil leaves and give the sauce a few stirs.

When the ravioli is done, drain it but allow a bit of moisture to cling to the ravioli when you throw it into the pan with the sauce. Toss until the ravioli is nicely coated, and then serve.

Tuna, Tomato, and Parsley Linguine

This is addictively good pasta. A quick, garlicky tomato sauce becomes a real dinner when combined with canned Italian tuna and tons of freshly chopped parsley. Most of the ingredients sit happily in the pantry until they're needed, so all you need to pick up on the way home is the garlic and parsley. Be sure to pick up the Italian oil-packed tuna—the flavor is much richer and tastier.

Makes 3 to 4 servings

1 (28-ounce) can whole Italian
　tomatoes
2 tablespoons extra-virgin olive oil
2 garlic cloves, minced
1 teaspoon kosher salt
½ teaspoon freshly ground
　black pepper
1 pound dried linguine
2 (6-ounce) cans Italian tuna packed
　in olive oil, drained well
½ cup finely chopped fresh parsley

Open the can of tomatoes and place it by the stove. Warm the olive oil and garlic over medium heat in a medium saucepan, stirring very often. The instant the garlic turns light gold, add the tomatoes and break them up with a spatula. Stir in the salt and pepper and let the sauce simmer for 20 to 25 minutes, until thickened.

Meanwhile, set a large pot of heavily salted water to boil and cook the linguine according to the package instructions. Drain.

When the sauce and pasta are ready, add the tuna to the tomato sauce and flake well with a fork. Stir in the parsley.

Toss the pasta with the sauce, then serve with extra parsley and pepper.

The Good, the Bad & the Yummy

Chicken Finger Quesadilla

Ah, the joy of the ultimate junk food: chicken tenders. No one needs to tell you to dip them in BBQ sauce, but if you're looking for a new way to make them really feel like dinner, bake them until they're crisp and fold them in a flour tortilla with a shower of Mexican cheeses and cilantro. Eat it quickly, while the chicken is still crunchy and the cheese is molten.

Makes 4 servings

1 (10-ounce) package frozen chicken fingers
4 flour tortillas
1 cup pre-shredded Mexican cheese blend, plus more for topping
½ cup finely chopped red onion
A bunch of cilantro leaves
Tabasco or Sriracha hot sauce to taste

Bake the chicken according to package directions.

When the chicken is ready, heat a large skillet over medium heat. Place one tortilla in the skillet and sprinkle half the cheese over the top. Nestle a few chicken tenders in the cheese, sprinkle with red onion, cilantro, and a couple dashes of hot sauce, and top with a little more cheese and another tortilla.

Let the quesadilla melt and lightly brown on one side, then use a wide spatula to flip it and brown the other side. Transfer the quesadilla to a plate and repeat to make the remaining quesadilla. Cut into wedges to serve.

RedHot Butter Shrimp

Hot sauce plus melted butter equals stinging hot bliss. Bake shrimp in the spicy butter for only a few minutes, and serve with plenty of crusty bread to soak up all the sauce and cool down your mouth.

Makes 3 to 4 servings

¼ pound (1 stick) unsalted butter
2 to 4 tablespoons Frank's RedHot sauce or Tabasco sauce
Kosher salt to taste
1 pound large shrimp, peeled but tail-on
Flat-leaf parsley, roughly chopped, to serve

Preheat the oven to 375°F. In a small saucepan, melt the butter and gradually whisk in the hot sauce. Season the sauce with salt to taste.

Arrange the shrimp in a medium (9-inch) casserole dish, and pour the sauce over them. Bake for 15 to 20 minutes, or until the shrimp are opaque and the sauce is sizzling.

Top with plenty of parsley and serve with hunks of bread.

Thai Basil Chicken

Track down some Thai red curry paste, boil some wide noodles, and get ready for this bright, glamorous, and oh-so-greasy bowl of pleasure.

Makes 3 to 4 servings

2 tablespoons vegetable oil

1 medium onion, thinly sliced

1 red pepper, seeded and thinly sliced

1 garlic clove, thinly sliced

1 pound ground chicken

1 tablespoon Thai red curry paste

1 cup canned coconut milk

1 cup loosely packed basil leaves, roughly torn

1 pound wide rice noodles or egg noodles

In a large wok or frying pan, heat the oil over medium-high heat. Add the onion and red pepper and cook until crisp-tender, about 5 minutes. Add the garlic and cook briefly, then stir in the ground chicken, breaking it up with a spatula as it cooks.

When the chicken is no longer pink, add the red curry paste and coconut milk, stirring until evenly combined. Simmer until the sauce is thickened and creamy. Add the basil and cook a couple minutes more.

Meanwhile, cook the noodles according to package directions, and drain thoroughly. Toss with the sauce and simmer in the pan for another minute or two.

Ramen Divine

Ordinarily, a cluster of average-tasting noodles and a foil packet of seasoning does not a delicious dinner make. So instead of pressuring ramen to be tasty all by its lonesome, give it some good company. Pack it with plenty of pan-fried tofu (or, for a truly trashy touch, Spam). Add crunch with sprouts. Top it off with something green like spinach or cilantro, and you're in business.

Chocolate Cake with Homemade Bittersweet Ganache

I've always been a fan of chocolate cake mixes. They call to me as I walk through the baking aisle, I give up and throw one in the cart, and I smile at the idea of spontaneous cake. It's good cake, too. Mixes go from powder to batter without fuss and they taste like chocolate. The only snag is the frosting. Commercial varieties might come from the same factory as the cake mixes, but they don't flatter the cake—they're often too thick and too artificial-tasting. Thank goodness for ganache. The name might sound as intimidating as hollandaise, but it's simply what the French call their shiny, dark mixture of warm cream and pure chocolate. It comes together in a few minutes on the stove, and then you get to pour it all over your fake-but-delicious cake. Divine.

Makes 1 (13 x 9-inch) sheet cake

1 package chocolate cake mix

1¼ cups heavy cream

12 ounces bittersweet chocolate, chopped

2 teaspoons vanilla extract

Prepare the cake mix according to package directions.

As the cake bakes, bring the cream to a gentle simmer in a heavy saucepan. Remove from the heat. Pile the chocolate into the saucepan and let sit for 5 minutes. Add the vanilla and whisk until smooth and shiny. Let cool in the fridge for 20 minutes to make it more spreadable, then frost your cake.

Caramelized Apple and Croissant Sundae

Even if dinner is a sack of takeout, dessert can be as comforting as something from grandma's oven. Just grab a couple of croissants from the bakery on the way home, sauté some apples, add a scoop of vanilla ice cream, and snuggle on the couch in front of the reality TV show no one else knows you love.

Makes 4 servings

2 croissants, split in half lengthwise

3 tablespoons unsalted butter

½ cup light brown sugar

Pinch of kosher salt

4 Granny Smith apples, peeled, cored, and cut into 6 wedges each

1 pint top-quality vanilla ice cream

Lightly toast the croissants.

In a large skillet over medium heat, melt the butter until foamy. Add the brown sugar and salt and stir with a spatula until melted and combined.

Add the apple wedges and sauté, turning frequently, until the apples are tender and perfumed.

Place a toasted croissant half in a bowl, and top with a scoop of ice cream, six of the apple wedges, and plenty of the apple-scented caramel. Repeat with the remaining three portions and serve right away.

Pigs in a Blanket, Anyone?

Sometimes the most sinful things come in the smallest packages. Take hors d'oeuvres, for instance. I don't know a single person who doesn't have a secret yearning for buttery, doughy, trashy treats like pigs in a blanket, mushroom puffs, mini egg rolls, and little curry beef pies. They exceed the deliciousness of almost every other item in the freezer case, and yet most people only think of them when they're giving a party. I say celebrate making it through the day and toss a boxful in the oven. Miniature snacks, especially outrageously rich ones, are so deliciously indulgent and silly that they'll bring a smile to your face. Set out some mustard, ketchup, and any other likely condiments, and eat them as a prelude to an equally sinful dinner, or throw caution to the wind and make a meal of the little darlings.

Whip It Good

We've all heard it before—olive oil is good for you; butter is the devil. In a world of heart-healthy spreads and butter-flavored sprays, sometimes only the real thing does the trick. Butter is divine in desserts and spread on bread, but it also happens to be an amazingly quick way to get a devilish dinner on the table in a hurry. Mix softened butter with vibrant flavors like rosemary, garlic, or blue cheese, and you have a ready-made flavoring for meat, fish, vegetables, and pasta. Fruit-flavored butters are perfect for roasted chicken and morning toast. These flavored butters will last a week or two in the fridge.

Garlic Butter: This is great with homemade garlic bread, melted over baked potatoes or mushrooms, or used to sauté shrimp. Just mix one stick of softened unsalted butter with one tablespoon minced garlic, one teaspoon salt, and a grinding of black pepper.

Fresh Herb Butter: This delicate butter adds lusciousness to baked fish, canned beans, and pasta. Mix one stick of softened unsalted butter with 1 tablespoon minced fresh herbs or one teaspoon dried herbs (rosemary, thyme, and oregano are all delicious), one teaspoon of salt, and one teaspoon grated lemon peel.

Cheese Butter: Toss this scrumptious butter with hot microwave popcorn, melt it over baked mushrooms, or slather on boiled corn. Mix one stick of softened unsalted butter with 1/4 cup grated cheese (Parmesan and Cheddar work well), 1/2 teaspoon salt, and 1/2 teaspoon paprika.

Sweet Fruit Butter: Perfect for hot, toasty muffins, bread, scones, and banana bread. Mix one stick of softened unsalted butter with 3 tablespoons of your favorite jam (strawberry, raspberry, and peach are divine) and a drop of vanilla extract.

CHAPTER 4

Mood Food

Sometimes, it's a harsh world out there. The chilly wind blows, piles of work accumulate, or life simply seems to be poking at you with a pointy stick. You need comfort, solace, relief. I'm guessing that, when this happens, cooking is the last thing on your mind. But don't pass the kitchen by too quickly. You'd be denying yourself a simple but nearly foolproof way of making yourself feel better.

Of course, there's no telling what kind of food might bring you comfort—for some, it's an obvious thing like grandma's chicken soup, for others, it's a strange guilty pleasure (mine's lima beans drenched in butter and salt). But no matter what you prefer, food has the ability to soothe old wounds and sustain you. Key the food to your mood and you're taking care of yourself, which is one step closer to feeling better.

Odds are, you'll find yourself craving one of two things: the clarity and healthfulness of Asian-style foods, or snuggly, comforting carbs. Either way, this chapter's got you covered.

¿

Go Good or Bad?

A QUICK DIAGNOSTIC QUIZ

if you

feel like you're walking on eggshells, be **Good**

have lost your stiff upper lip, be **Bad**

hunger for some peace and quiet, be **Good**

find yourself tearing up at Disney movie commercials, be **Bad**

daydream about bubble baths, be **Good**

?

good TEMPLE CALM

It might seem silly to suggest that food can bring you serenity. After all, isn't raiding the fridge when you're feeling upset a sure way to make you feel bad about yourself? Nutritionists advise you to take a walk instead, or knit a scarf, but though those are good ideas, they miss the point. Eating when you're upset doesn't have to mean eating something loaded with carbs or calories. Cradling a bowl of clear, steaming broth or a lovingly made cup of tea can bring an alert, calm peacefulness that's just as satisfying.

Not surprisingly, Japanese-style foods seem to bring out the inner Buddha more than anything else. Aromatic soups, dumplings, fish, and rice give your body the balance and lightness it needs to re-establish equilibrium. For maximum effect, breathe in the aromas as you cook your food. Serve it on your best china. Savor each sip, bite slowly, and nourish yourself, body and soul.

Chinese-Jewish Chicken Soup

There's never a wrong time to eat chicken soup, but when you're feeling the weight of the world on your shoulders, it's ideal. Cupping your hands around a bowl of steaming hot broth is the more nourishing equivalent of tossing back a stiff drink to "steady the nerves." The best version I've ever had was my grandmother's, of course, with plenty of matzo balls and dill. But since I can never get my soup to taste like hers, I make mine Asian-inflected instead. The shitakes (which rival the portobello for the title of meatiest mushroom) add a savory depth to the broth, and watercress makes it look lovely. Cook up a massive pot, and keep sipping until you feel better. The boiled chicken has a soft texture that's also very comforting.

Makes 6 to 8 servings

2½ pounds chicken wings, legs, and/or thighs (preferably organic)

10 cups water

¾ cup rice wine or sake

6 slices ginger, smashed with the flat side of a knife

1 small bunch scallions, trimmed and cut in half

1 star anise (optional)

10 shitake mushrooms, thinly sliced

1 bunch watercress, washed well and trimmed

Rinse the chicken pieces under cold water, then place them in a big pot with the water, rice wine or sake, ginger, scallions, and star anise. Bring to a boil and then reduce the heat to low and simmer for 1½ hours, skimming off any foam that's released early on.

Strain the broth, reserving the chicken pieces. Return the broth and chicken to the pot. Add the mushrooms and watercress and simmer over medium heat for 5 minutes, until the shitakes are tender and the watercress is bright green.

Soothing Rice Congee

Like all the best comfort foods, Chinese rice congee (also called jook or porridge) is gentle but never bland. Like chicken soup, it's legendary for its healing properties, and its soothing texture and delicate taste is an ideal source of nourishment if you're feeling under the weather. Only a small amount of rice is needed in proportion to the chicken broth, since the rice expands and dissolves when it's cooked in lots of broth. The toppings add extra vibrancy and flavor, but the congee is just as delicious plain.

Makes 6 to 8 servings

8 cups canned low-sodium
   chicken broth

1 cup long-grain rice

2 teaspoons julienned fresh ginger

Kosher salt, to taste

½ teaspoon ground white pepper

TOPPINGS

Shredded cooked chicken

Cilantro and scallions, roughly
   chopped

Sesame oil

Soy sauce

Heat the broth in a large pot until simmering, then add the rice. Reduce the heat until the broth is barely simmering, then cook for 1½ hours, stirring occasionally. Add the ginger and simmer for 20 minutes more, or until the congee has the consistency of thick barley soup. Taste and add salt, if necessary, and the white pepper. The congee should taste delicate, but never bland.

Ladle the congee into bowls, and garnish with whatever toppings you'd like.

Zen Dumplings

Though Freud and his cohorts would disagree, sometimes the best thing to do when you're stressed isn't to just talk about it, but to do something. Something methodical, repetitive, and relaxing can often help. For some, yoga, meditation, or knitting fit the bill, but cooking can have rhythms that are just as calming. Filling and crimping neat rows of petite vegetarian dumplings leaves you feeling soothed, focused, and surprisingly industrious. Freeze any extra dumplings for a soothing snack with a cup of tea. You'll need a steamer insert to cook the dumplings.

Makes 35 dumplings

6 whole dried shitake mushrooms

1 (5-ounce) package baked tofu, teriyaki flavor, drained

2 tablespoons finely chopped scallions

1 teaspoon finely minced ginger

½ cup canned water chestnuts, drained and finely chopped

½ cup coarsely grated carrots

2 teaspoons soy sauce

½ teaspoon toasted sesame oil

½ teaspoon kosher salt

35 wonton wrappers

Soy sauce mixed with water or rice vinegar, for dipping

To make the dumpling filling, soak the shitake mushrooms in a small bowl of hot water until tender and pliable, about 15 minutes. Chop them finely and place in a large bowl. Cut the tofu into ¼-inch cubes and add to the bowl along with the scallions, ginger, water chestnuts, carrots, soy sauce, sesame oil, and salt. Toss together gently and taste. The flavor should be earthy but delicate—add more soy sauce or sesame oil if you'd think it needs it.

To maximize the relaxing, methodical benefits of creating these dumplings, create an assembly line of dumpling components before you begin: wonton wrappers, a big bowl of filling with a small spoon, a small bowl of water, and a tray lined with wax paper on which to arrange the dumplings.

Next, form the dumplings. Drop a teaspoon of filling into the center of a wonton skin, being careful not to let the filling touch the edges of the wonton wrapper. Dip a finger into the water bowl and moisten the edges of the dough, then fold the wrapper in half. Fold or crimp the edges 6 to 8 times to seal. Don't worry if they don't look perfect. Repeat with the remaining filling and wonton wrappers.

In a large saucepan, bring about an inch of water to a gentle simmer. Lightly grease the steamer insert with vegetable oil, and place in the saucepan. Arrange a single layer of dumplings in the steamer. Steam for 12 minutes, until the filling is hot and the wrappers are fully cooked. Repeat.

Glass Noodle Salad with Tofu and Lime

In Chinese folklore, noodles represent longevity. For us, they also mean no-stress cooking. Unlike most noodles, glass noodles become fully cooked when boiling water is poured over them. Toss them with a sesame-soy dressing, baked tofu, sprouts, and cilantro, and serve warm or cold with plenty of sesame seeds on top. You can find glass noodles in the Asian section of the supermarket, also labeled as bean thread or cellophane noodles. Be sure to get the kind that's as thin as angel hair pasta.

Makes 3 to 4 servings

FOR THE SAUCE

1 tablespoon Chinese sesame oil

2 tablespoons soy sauce

2 teaspoons rice vinegar

1 large garlic clove, minced

1 teaspoon minced fresh ginger

1 teaspoon sugar

FOR THE SALAD

2 ounces thin glass noodles

½ pound bean sprouts

1 (8-ounce) package baked tofu (your favorite flavor), thinly sliced

1 carrot, peeled and thinly sliced into shreds

2 tablespoons chopped cilantro

2 teaspoons toasted sesame seeds (optional)

First, make the sauce by whisking all of the sauce ingredients together in a small bowl. Set aside to let the flavors meld together.

In a medium saucepan, bring 4 cups of water to a boil. Place the glass noodles in a large bowl. Add the bean sprouts to the saucepan and cook for 1 minute. Drain the bean sprouts, reserving the hot water. Run some cold water over the sprouts, and place them in another large bowl.

Pour the reserved hot water over the glass noodles and let them sit for just 15 to 30 seconds, or until tender but still al dente. Drain the noodles and return them to their bowl. Toss them with the sauce, pulling apart any clumps with two forks. Add the bean sprouts, tofu, carrots, and cilantro and toss again. Serve topped with the sesame seeds.

Tokyo Shrimp in Green Tea Broth

For edible solace and support, there's nothing better than hunching over a big, steaming bowl of noodles, shrimp, and vegetables, topped with a forest of fresh herbs. The abundance makes you feel cared for, especially since you're eating something good for you.

Makes 2 servings

½ pound large shrimp, shell on

2 tablespoons rice wine or sake

1 teaspoon minced fresh ginger

4 cups homemade or canned
   low-sodium chicken broth

2 tablespoons sweetened rice wine

2 tablespoons soy sauce

2 carrots, peeled and julienned

2 cup mung bean sprouts

½ pound udon or soba noodles

A handful of cilantro leaves

Peel the shrimp, reserving the shells and leaving the tails on the shrimp. Devein the shrimp and place them in a bowl with the rice wine and ginger, and toss to coat.

Simmer the chicken broth in a medium saucepan with the reserved shrimp shells, sweetened rice wine, and soy sauce for 10 minutes, then strain the broth. Add the carrots, bean sprouts, and shrimp to the strained broth and simmer for a couple minutes more.

In a large pot, bring plenty of water to a boil and cook the udon or soba noodles according to package directions. Drain and add to the soup, then serve topped with cilantro.

Sliced Chicken with Chinese Broccoli and Spicy Soy

This slow-cooked chicken yields juicy meat with only a few moments of effort. Start the chicken as soon as you come home from a long day at the office—it takes about 2 hours to cook, but it's hands-off time. Add crunch and freshness with Chinese broccoli and flavor with a simple soy dipping sauce. Leftovers are delicious straight from the fridge.

Makes 3 to 4 servings

1½ pounds chicken breasts, skin on
   and bone in

1 scallion, roughly chopped

3 thick slices fresh ginger

½ teaspoon whole black peppercorns

1 pound Chinese broccoli, trimmed

Soy sauce and Chinese sesame oil
   to taste

Place the chicken in a medium-size, heavy pot and add enough water to cover it by 2 inches. Add the scallion, ginger, and peppercorns, and bring the water to a strong boil over high heat. Turn off the heat, cover the pot, and let it sit unattended for at least 2 hours, until fully cooked.

Remove the cooked chicken from the pot and set aside. Bring the liquid in the pot to a boil again and add the Chinese broccoli. Cook for 5 minutes and drain.

Meanwhile, peel off the chicken's skin and pull the breast meat off the bones. Slice the chicken against the grain into 1-inch-thick pieces.

Whisk together a few drops of soy sauce and sesame oil, and use as a drizzle or dipping sauce for the chicken and the broccoli.

Miso Sea Bass with Shitakes

Heat is serene—and not just at the sauna. Cooking sea bass or any other firm white fish with gentle oven heat instead of the harsh heat of the grill or skillet means truly tender, aromatic fish without the need for additional fat. Shitakes have long been prized in Asian cultures for their disease-fighting abilities, but their earthy taste also adds a comforting touch to seafood. Part of the serenity of this dish is its ease—just spread the fish with the miso paste, bake with the shitakes, and in less than 15 minutes, your simple piece of fish is ready. If you'd like, you can marinate the salmon with the miso paste for up to 4 hours. For a more substantial meal, serve with steamed bok choy and/or rice.

Makes 2 servings

FOR THE MISO PASTE

3 tablespoons light miso

1½ tablespoons sake

2 teaspoons sugar

1 teaspoon grated fresh ginger

1 teaspoon grated orange peel

2 teaspoons orange juice

FOR THE FISH

2 (6-ounce) salmon filets, skin on

12 shitake mushrooms, stemmed

If you're baking the fish right away, preheat the oven to broil and set the rack and a baking sheet in the middle of the oven. If you're marinating it first, preheat the oven when you're ready to bake the fish.

Combine the miso paste ingredients together in a wide bowl and add the salmon filets and shitakes, turning both several times to cover. If you'd like, marinate the fish, covered, in the refrigerator for up to four hours.

Remove the hot baking tray from the oven and coat it with nonstick cooking spray or a bit of vegetable oil. Place the shitakes in a pile in the center of the baking sheet, with the two salmon filets skin-side up alongside. Broil until the salmon skin looks crispy and the shitakes look cooked, about 8 minutes. Remove from the oven and serve.

Chai-Spiced Tapioca Pudding

I love chai spices like cinnamon, cardamom, cloves, and black pepper—they manage to taste exotic and comforting at the same time. So why only use them to make chai? Extend their nurturing powers by pairing them with that comfort-food classic, tapioca pudding. Using soy milk instead of cow's milk makes it even healthier.

Makes 3 to 4 servings

3 cups low-fat soy milk

A pinch of kosher salt

4 cardamom pods, lightly crushed

2 cloves

½ cinnamon stick

8 black peppercorns

¼ cup small pearl tapioca

½ cup sugar

1 teaspoon vanilla extract

Pour the soy milk into a large saucepan and add the salt, cardamom, cloves, cinnamon, and peppercorns. Simmer for 5 minutes, then turn off the heat and let the spices infuse into the soy milk for 10 to 15 minutes. Strain out the spices and return the soy milk to the saucepan.

Add the tapioca, sugar, and vanilla and simmer uncovered for 10 to 15 minutes, until the tapioca is al dente and translucent and the pudding has thickened. Eat the pudding while it's still warm, or chill it in a large bowl or individual cups before serving.

The Soup Doctor is IN

Soup may be a great antidote for stress, but if you're too exasperated or impatient to make it, don't put yourself through the rigmarole of cooking it from scratch. Instead, doctor up canned or boxed broths and you'll have a lovely soup in a matter of minutes.

Instant Wonton. Simmer chicken broth with a few slices of fresh ginger, a bit of chopped scallion, and 4 or 5 frozen wontons or dumplings. Garnish with a few drops of toasted sesame oil.

Instant Greek Egg Drop. Simmer chicken broth with a pinch of dried oregano for a few minutes, then add a beaten egg that's been whisked with a squeeze of lemon. Swirl with a fork just until cooked through. Garnish with freshly ground black pepper.

Instant Fresh Pea. Simmer canned chicken broth with an equal volume of frozen peas until hot. Blend with an immersion blender and serve hot or cold with a swirl of yogurt or sour cream.

Instant Curried Split Pea. In a small saucepan, heat a small pat of butter with a small handful of finely chopped onion or shallot and sauté until golden. Add pinches of ground cumin, coriander, and cayenne and stir constantly until fragrant. Add canned split pea soup and simmer for 5 to 10 minutes, then serve.

Instant Coconut Corn. Heat boxed creamy corn soup with a few slices of fresh ginger and a couple glugs of canned coconut milk. Throw in some raw or frozen shrimp if you like. Simmer for 5 to 10 minutes, then top with freshly chopped cilantro.

—bad⇄

CARB COMFORT

Oh wondrous, wondrous carbs. Healers of wounds, soothers of souls. If you need a dose of comfort, just watch a pat of butter melt over a tangle of tagliatelle—suddenly, all is right with the world. Sure, we could lose ourselves in stiff cocktails or marathon sessions of bad TV, but those activities merely bring solace. Diving into comfort food brings pleasure.

Unlike other foods, carbs seduce more by texture than by taste. There's the slightly leathery crust of a roasted potato spear and the cashmere smoothness of a potato puree. The rich creaminess of a good risotto or the gentle chewiness of fried rice. In fact, it's almost the *absence* of intense flavor that helps make carbs so comforting. Simple-tasting foods feel like home. Maybe that's why diving into a warm bread basket can be even more gratifying than sampling an exotic curry. So forget about your diet-conscious carb-phobia and give in to a big plate of love.

Smoky Corn Chowder with Bacon and Leeks

This shamelessly creamy soup is sweet, salty, and oniony. The combination of crumbled bacon, silky strands of leek, crunchy corn kernels, and soft cubes of potato creates comfort food perfection. 'Nuff said.

Makes 4 to 6 servings

2 tablespoons unsalted butter

½ cup chopped bacon, divided

1 cup finely chopped onion

2 fat leeks, sliced in half, washed, and white part thinly sliced

1 celery stalk, thinly sliced

2 teaspoons fresh thyme leaves

4 cups frozen corn kernels

1 cup peeled and diced Yukon Gold potato

2 cups whole milk

Kosher salt and freshly ground black pepper

A pinch of cayenne pepper

In a large saucepan, heat the butter and ¼ cup of the chopped bacon until the fat renders out of the bacon. Add the onion, leeks, celery, and thyme and sauté until the onion is translucent and tender.

Add the corn, potato, and milk and simmer for 15 minutes, or until the potato chunks are tender. Season with salt, pepper, and cayenne.

In a small frying pan, fry the remaining bacon until crisp, then crumble over each bowl of soup.

Spaghetti Carbonara

Spaghetti carbonara means "coal-miner's spaghetti," but the name could easily be referring to the comforting, carb-heavy richness of the dish. In fact, the rough, deprived life of a coal miner couldn't be further from the sheer luxury of a good carbonara. This sauce has no tomatoes or meatballs—just a rich sauce of eggs, bacon, and Pecorino Romano cheese that glossily coats the strands of spaghetti. Take care not to overcook the sauce—you want it to be creamy, not scrambled.

Makes 4 servings

5 tablespoons extra-virgin olive oil

5 slices bacon, roughly chopped

4 large eggs, at room temperature

½ cup fresh, good-quality ricotta, at room temperature

1 pound spaghetti

Kosher salt

¾ cup frozen green peas

½ cup grated Pecorino Romano cheese

Coarsely ground black pepper

Heat the olive oil and bacon together in a large skillet over low heat so that the fat from the bacon starts to melt. Meanwhile, beat the eggs and ricotta together and set aside.

Cook the pasta in boiling salted water until almost al dente. When the pasta is about a minute from being done, add the peas to the pasta pot and raise the heat under the bacon pan. Cook the bacon until it just starts to become crispy, then remove the pan from the heat.

Drain the pasta and peas and add them to the bacon pan along with the beaten ricotta mixture, most of the Pecorino Romano cheese, and lots of coarsely ground black pepper. Quickly toss the pasta with the sauce ingredients, so the heat of the pasta slightly cooks the eggs.

Serve topped with the remaining Pecorino Romano cheese and extra black pepper.

Tater Tot Bake with Mozzarella and Spicy Marinara

I've always had a weakness for tater tots. The addiction might come from childhood fast-food break-fasts with my mom, where my sister and I consumed an almost unbelievable number of hash browns without any apparent ill effects. Now that I'm older, I still hanker for crunchy potatoes when I want to coddle myself, but I'm not content to merely toss a few frozen pieces onto a baking sheet. Instead, I like to cover them in homemade tomato sauce and mozzarella in a kind of Italian-inspired potato gratin. It might sound like overkill (and of course it is), but what the tater tots lose in crunchiness, I gain in sheer comfort.

Makes 6 to 8 servings

1 (32-ounce) package frozen tater tots

2 tablespoons extra-virgin olive oil

½ cup finely chopped onion

2 garlic cloves, minced

1 (28-ounce) can whole tomatoes

½ teaspoon kosher salt,
   plus more to taste

A few grindings of black pepper,
   plus more to taste

½ teaspoon crushed red pepper flakes

2 cups shredded mozzarella

Bake the tater tots according to package directions, removing the potatoes from the oven a few minutes before they're golden brown.

Meanwhile, heat the olive oil in a medium saucepan over medium-high heat, and fry the onions until tender and light gold. Add the garlic and cook, stirring constantly, for about 30 seconds. Add the tomatoes, breaking them up with a spatula. Add the salt, pepper, and red pepper flakes and bring the sauce to a simmer. Reduce the heat to medium-low and simmer the sauce until slightly thickened, about 30 to 40 minutes. Adjust the seasonings if you like.

Preheat the oven to 375°F. In a large, wide baking dish, layer half of the tater tots with half of the tomato sauce and half of the mozzarella. Repeat to form the second layer, and top the mozzarella with a few grindings of pepper. Bake for 25 to 30 minutes, until the cheese is bubbling and golden brown. Let cool before eating.

Fondue with Kielbasa, Apples, and Baguette

Anyone who says that fondue went out of fashion along with platform heels is being a bit unfair. Fondue is no fad—the Swiss were dipping food in melted cheese long before the disco era, and it's still a perfectly sensible idea. How could it not be? Everything tastes better dipped in cheese, and fondue only takes 10 minutes to make. Fondue pots are cheap, and so is Sterno. The key is treating fondue like a melted cheese plate. Only good Gruyère and Emmenthaler are worthy of the fondue pot. Pair them with foods that complement the cheese but are also sturdy enough to withstand the dipping process. Firm fruits like apples and pears work great, nectarines and oranges don't. Challah bread would drown, while baguettes and whole grain breads stand their ground. And while sausages are too heavy for dipping in cheese, and prosciutto is too light, kielbasa is just perfect—smoky, juicy, and not too rich.

Makes 4 to 6 servings

FOR THE FONDUE

1 garlic clove, peeled

2 cups dry white wine

2 teaspoons cornstarch

2 tablespoons kirsch (cherry brandy)
   or water

½ pound Emmenthaler cheese,
   coarsely grated

½ pound Gruyère cheese,
   coarsely grated

Kosher salt and freshly ground pepper

FOR DIPPING

2 to 3 tart apples, sliced

2 crusty baguettes, thinly sliced

½ pound kielbasa, cut into chunks

In a medium saucepan, combine the garlic and the wine and bring to a boil over medium-high heat. Cook for 3 minutes to evaporate the alcohol, being careful not to ignite the alcohol. Remove the garlic.

In a small bowl, combine the cornstarch and the kirsch or water until smooth, then whisk the mixture into the wine. Add both types of cheese to the pot and reduce the heat to medium-low, stirring the fondue with a wooden spoon until the cheese dissolves, about 5 minutes. Season to taste with salt and pepper.

Set out plates with the apples, baguette, and kielbasa. Pour the fondue into the fondue pot and set the Sterno to its lowest flame. Dip everything in the fondue and enjoy the cheesiness.

Indian-Spiced Shepherd's Pie

Simmered with cinnamon, clove, cardamom, and black pepper, this slightly atypical version of shepherd's pie fills the whole kitchen with aroma as it bakes, and nothing is more comforting on a blustery day. Running a fork over the buttery mashed potato topping is inexplicably fun, and also increases the crunchiness of the end result. This tastes even better as it sits, and a square of it makes a perfect lunch.

Makes 4 to 6 servings

FOR THE MEAT FILLING

3 tablespoons vegetable oil

5 whole cloves

¼ teaspoon whole black peppercorns

¼ teaspoon whole cumin seeds

1 cinnamon stick

3 cardamom pods

2 bay leaves

2 medium onions, chopped

2 cups peeled and chopped tomatoes

2 teaspoons hot curry powder

1 pound ground lamb or beef

¾ teaspoon kosher salt

FOR THE POTATO TOPPING

1½ pounds Yukon Gold potatoes

½ cup heavy cream

1 cup whole milk

2 tablespoons unsalted butter

Kosher salt and freshly ground pepper

1 large egg, lightly beaten

In a large skillet, heat the oil over medium-high heat. Add the cloves, peppercorns, cumin, cinnamon stick, cardamom, and bay leaves. When the bay leaves darken a bit, add the onions and cook, stirring occasionally, until they turn a bit brown. Add the tomatoes and cook until they break down into a paste, then add the curry powder and stir constantly for 1 minute.

Add the lamb or beef and cook, breaking up clumps with your spatula, until the meat is no longer pink. Add 1 cup of water and the salt, then bring to a boil. Reduce the heat to medium-low, cover the pan, and let the meat curry simmer for about 30 minutes, until the flavors blend. Remove the lid, raise the heat, and boil off any excess liquid. Pick out the whole spices and throw them away.

Meanwhile, cook the potatoes: bring a large pot of salted water to a boil, then add the potatoes and cook until fork tender, about 20 to 30 minutes.

Heat the cream, milk, and butter in a medium saucepan along with a generous dose of salt and pepper. Drain the potatoes, and when they are cool enough to handle, peel them and mash them with the heated cream mixture and the beaten egg. Add more salt and pepper if you like.

Preheat the oven to 375°F. Spread the meat curry in an even layer in a 13 x 9-inch pan. Use a rubber spatula to spread the mashed potato over the meat, then run a fork over the top in a squiggly design. Bake for 35 to 40 minutes, until the shepherd's pie is very hot and the potato crust is golden brown.

Chocolate-Apple Brown Betty

When the cold wind blows and you want pure nursery-style comfort, it's time to stay inside and pull something buttery and old-fashioned out of the oven. An apple betty is perfect—no dough to fuss over, just sugary buttered crumbs topping soft fruit. And it's a classic dessert that brings soulful comfort. Chunks of dark chocolate add a dose of extra richness, melting in the heat and soaking into the crumbs and fruit. Make the breadcrumbs by pulverizing fresh or slightly stale white bread in a food processor or spice grinder.

Makes 4 to 6 servings

FOR THE APPLES

3 tart apples, peeled and cored

2 tablespoons unsalted butter

FOR THE BUTTERY CRUMBS

¾ cup soft white breadcrumbs

1 cup light brown sugar

3½ ounces dark chocolate,
   roughly chopped

5 tablespoons unsalted butter

3 tablespoons pure maple syrup

Preheat the oven to 375°F. Cut the apples into chunks and place them in a medium pan with the butter and a couple tablespoons of water over medium heat. Cook, stirring occasionally, for 8 to 10 minutes, until the apples just begin to soften but are still holding their shape. Tip the apples and their juices into a medium-sized baking dish.

In a medium bowl, mix the breadcrumbs, brown sugar, and chocolate chunks and cover the apples with the mixture. In a small saucepan, melt the butter with the maple syrup and transfer to a liquid measuring cup. Drizzle the buttery syrup evenly over the crumb topping, trying to saturate as much of it as possible.

Bake for 30 to 35 minutes, or until the crumbs are golden but not yet brown.

Strawberry and Mascarpone Risotto

Risottos are traditionally savory, but they don't need to be. This one makes the most of the affinity between strawberries and mascarpone cheese, with a drizzle of balsamic vinegar to add depth and a bit of bite. If you're looking for comfort food with a bit of edge, this grown-up rice pudding is it.

Makes 4 servings

¾ cup arborio rice

2½ to 3 cups whole milk (do not substitute low-fat or skim milk)

½ cup plus 2 tablespoons sugar

½ teaspoon grated orange zest

1 vanilla bean, split, or 1 teaspoon vanilla extract

½ cup chopped ripe strawberries

½ cup mascarpone cheese, at room temperature

Balsamic vinegar

In a heavy-bottomed large saucepan, combine the rice, 2½ cups of milk, the sugar, and orange zest. Scrape the seeds from the vanilla bean into the pot, and then toss in the pod.

Heat the rice over medium-low heat and stir until the liquid just begins to bubble. Reduce the heat so the risotto cooks at a gentle simmer. Cook for 30 to 40 minutes, stirring frequently with a wooden spoon, until the pudding is thick and creamy, and the rice is tender and soft. If the risotto needs more liquid, add a bit more milk as it cooks.

Gently fold the strawberries and mascarpone into the risotto, drizzle with some good balsamic vinegar, and dig in right away, while the strawberries have that great firm-soft texture.

International Bubbles

There's something about Champagne. The festive pop of the cork, the friendly fizz, and the bracing taste all conspire together to lift your spirits (the alcohol content doesn't hurt, either). But Champagne shouldn't be reserved only for celebrations. Its mood-boosting qualities make it a perfect mid-week pick-me-up. The trick? Finding a bottle that tastes great but has the price of an everyday wine. The key is looking beyond France. Plenty of other countries make terrific bubbly wines that taste terrific but don't cost as much as Champagne.

Spain: Cava is produced with the same *méthode champenoise* used to make Champagne. It's best when it's young, while it still keeps its fruitiness. Look for Brut Nature or Extra Brut designations to avoid excess sweetness.

Italy: Prosecco is made in the Veneto region just north of Venice, and boasts a nice bitter finish that makes it ideal for people who hate cloying sparkling wines. It's also great mixed with peach juice to make a Bellini.

Portugal: Vinho Verde can be either red or white, though in America we usually only see the whites on the shelves. White Vinho Verde is a simple and crisp, very refreshing in the summer and great with seafood and chicken. Like Spanish Cava, it's best enjoyed when it is young, so look for last year's vintage.

Germany: Keep an eye out for Deutscher Sekt, which is bottle-fermented from high-quality, single-estate German wines. The best ones are made from Riesling, Pinot Noir, or Pinot Gris grapes.

The Good, the Bad & the Yummy

Triple-Crème Time

Even straight from the fridge, good cheese is a balm for the soul. I find myself lingering in cheese shops much more often in winter than summer—that's when I seem to crave all that milky goodness. So it's lucky that some of the best, richest cheeses are at their peak when the weather is at its worst. Rich, aged, semisoft cow's milk cheeses usually have the most wintry richness (goat and sheep's milk cheeses tend to be lower in fat) but don't forget about ultra-rich fresh triple-cream goat cheeses. Try these winter cheeses, melted on toast or eaten at room temperature with simple foods like hot boiled potatoes, pickles, onions, and good beer.

Morbier
A full-bodied, semisoft, raw-milk cheese from the Franche-Comté region of France.

Raclette
A Swiss Alpine cheese that's similar to Gruyère—nutty, slightly sweet, and dotted with small holes. Terrific for melting.

Taleggio
A rich, almost pungent Italian cheese from the Lombardy region with a pinkish-orange washed rind. Delicious alone or tossed with hot pasta.

Reblochon
A creamy-soft French cheese with a dark golden, moldy rind, Reblochon is sold in small disks. The warm, yeasty aroma is delicate and reminiscent of walnuts.

Triple-Crème Goat Cheese
Sweeter and more delicate than mascarpone, these extra-rich goat cheeses hold their own against their more pungent counterparts.

Hot and Alcoholic

Mixing up a warm spiked cocktail is almost as retro as fondue, and just as comforting. Nothing warms you up faster, and a hot toddy does actually make you feel better when you're stuffed up. All these recipes make enough for two.

For a hot toddy, mix ½ cup bourbon with 1 teaspoon honey, ½ cup boiling water, and a squeeze of fresh lemon juice.

For spiked hot chocolate, add ½ cup whole milk to a medium saucepan along with 2 tablespoons natural cocoa powder (preferably Scharffen Berger) and ¼ cup sugar, and heat over medium heat, stirring until the mixture is smooth. Stir in another ½ cup of milk and 3 to 4 tablespoons rum or brandy, and heat until nice and steaming (but not boiling).

For hot buttered rum, divide 2 teaspoons sugar, 2 pats of butter, ¼ cup dark rum, and 8 cloves between two mugs. Add a cup of boiling water to each mug, then stir thoroughly.

For a hot, boozy cider, heat 1⅓ cups water, 2 cinnamon sticks, 3 to 4 cloves, 1 large piece of orange peel, 2½ tablespoons light brown sugar, ⅔ cup apple cider, and ½ cup light or spiced rum in a medium saucepan over medium-low heat for 5 to 10 minutes to infuse, then serve.

CHAPTER 5:

Party Time

A party can be the easiest thing in the world: just get a bunch of friends together, a bottle of wine (or a couple of forties) and no game plan. But when you're playing host, you can do much more than provide booze. You can be positively Machiavellian. The mood of the party is in your hands.

Do you feel like an elegant afternoon affair, or a party that starts at 10 p.m. and ends with breakfast? Should people get dressed up or just show up? Would you prefer a party with guys or a party where you girls just talk about guys? Do you want to get flat-out sloshed or simply sip? Pay attention to your mood, and you'll soon discover what kind of celebration you'd like best.

The answers to these questions lead straight to what kind of food you'll serve. An elegant, girls-only gathering calls for light canapés, while a party demands shamelessly trashy, indulgent food. You'll find a party to fit each inclination in the pages that follow.

¿

Go Good or Bad?

A QUICK DIAGNOSTIC QUIZ

if you

want to be a lady who lunches, be Good

are climbing the walls of your balanced diet, be Bad

need an excuse to eat fried chicken, be Bad

yearn to listen to Sade and Vivaldi, be Good

ache for some down-home crunk or Chuck Berry, be Bad

?

good SPA SOCIAL

Everyone could use a little pampering, darling—and there's no need to press yourself longingly against the window of a spa if you crave it. Gather with your friends for a girls-only beauty day, complete with a refreshing spa spread to nosh on before you whip out the facial masks. Just like a good yoga or meditation session, getting massages, manicures, and really spiffy haircuts can help you feel cared for and honored.

Get as elegant or as goofy as you want. Give each other bad French manicures or run around in curlers. Stay sober with mango iced tea or knock back Pimm's Cups and get sloshy. Set out a tray of dainty snacks that demand to be eaten with pinkies up. Whatever you do, you'll revel in an activity you might not have engaged in since junior high—girl bonding.

Vanilla Mango Iced Tea

Iced tea has long been the preferred drink for refined ladylike refreshment, but it can get a little dull. This version, infused with chunks of mango and chopped vanilla bean, is a refreshing alternative that beats the pants off of lame bottled teas flavored with fake flavor extracts.

Makes 8 cups

6 English Breakfast tea bags

$\frac{2}{3}$ cup sugar

1 vanilla bean

2 mangoes, peeled, pitted, and cut into large cubes

1 cup mango nectar

Bring 8 cups of water to a boil, then pour over the tea bags in a large bowl. Infuse the tea until it's a bit stronger than usual, then remove the tea bags and let the tea cool.

In a medium saucepan, combine the sugar with $\frac{1}{4}$ cup of water. With a small, sharp knife, split the vanilla bean lengthwise. Scrape out the seeds and add them to the sugar mixture. Roughly chop the vanilla bean and add it to the pot as well. Bring the sugar mixture to a boil, reduce the heat, and simmer, stirring occasionally, until a clear syrup flecked with vanilla forms. Set the vanilla syrup aside to cool.

Strain the vanilla syrup through a sieve to remove the vanilla chunks (the pretty seeds remain in the syrup). Mix the vanilla syrup, cubed mango, and mango nectar with the cooled tea. Transfer the tea to a pitcher and chill before serving over ice.

Pimm's Cups

This is a drink that manages to be inebriating and elegant at the same time. Pimm's Cup is a classic English drink, meant to be sipped by demure ladies on hot afternoons while watching the boys play tennis. Cucumber spears and a splash of ginger ale add refreshing flavor to the caramel-ish taste of Pimm's No. 1 liquor.

Makes 8 to 10 servings

2 cups Pimm's No. 1 liquor
2 cups lemonade, chilled
3 cups ginger ale, chilled
Cucumber spears, for garnish

In a pitcher, combine the Pimm's, lemonade, and ginger ale. For each serving, pour the mixture over an ice-filled glass and garnish with a cucumber spear.

Melon, Prosciutto, and Mint Canapés

There's no need to turn on the oven or call for takeout when you want to feed your hungry friends. Just stock your kitchen with cantaloupe melon, good prosciutto, fresh mint, and baguettes and you have the makings of a lunch so elegant it begs to be eaten with pinkies up. Cantaloupe melon is also high in Vitamin A, which is known to support healthy skin, and olive oil helps keep the skin supple.

Makes 6 to 8 servings

1 small baguette, cut into ½-inch-thick slices (about 30 to 40 slices)

Extra-virgin olive oil

Kosher salt and freshly ground pepper

½ pound imported prosciutto, thinly sliced

2 cups cantaloupe melon chunks, thinly sliced

1 tablespoon finely chopped fresh mint

Preheat the oven to 325°F. Arrange the baguette slices on a large baking sheet and brush them lightly with olive oil. Sprinkle with salt and pepper to taste. Toast in the oven for 5 to 10 minutes, or until just barely golden.

Meanwhile, tear each slice of prosciutto into 3 or 4 pieces. Toss the melon in a small bowl with the mint.

When the baguette slices have toasted, remove them to a serving platter. Top each baguette toast with one or two slices of cantaloupe and a scrunched-up piece of prosciutto, and serve warm or at room temperature.

Lemony Ricotta and Herb Dip with Crudités

There's a reason why dips are popular at parties—dunking vegetables into a shared bowl of dip is almost as communal as fondue. This one—creamy, herby, and tart—manages to be light and luscious. For the best texture, buy fresh ricotta from a cheese store or Italian shop, or drain supermarket ricotta in a cheesecloth overnight.

Makes 6 to 8 servings

2 tablespoons extra-virgin olive oil,
　plus more to taste
¾ cup finely chopped onion
1½ cups ricotta cheese
½ cup light cream cheese,
　at room temperature
2 tablespoons finely chopped fresh
　herbs, a combination of your
　choice of dill, basil, oregano,
　and/or parsley
1 teaspoon grated lemon peel
1 tablespoon freshly squeezed
　lemon juice
Kosher salt and freshly ground black
　pepper, to taste
Assorted crudités to serve: cherry
　tomatoes, zucchini spears, baby
　carrots, and blanched broccoli

In a medium skillet, heat the olive oil over medium heat and add the onion. Cook, stirring occasionally, until the onion turns deeply golden and tender, about 15 minutes.

Transfer the onions to a blender and add the ricotta, cream cheese, herbs, lemon peel, and lemon juice. Blend until just slightly textured. Season with salt and pepper and add a drizzle of olive oil if you like, then blend again.

Serve the ricotta dip with the crudités.

Cool Pea and Arugula Soup

Peas may be available year-round in your grocer's freezer, but they still taste best in the summer, especially when pureed into this creamy, electric-green soup. The best peas come from a good farmer's market—taste a few to be sure they're sweet and not starchy. If you can't make it to the market, frozen peas usually taste sweeter than the fresh ones in the produce section. Podding all those peas may seem like a hassle if you do it standing at the counter, so relax at the kitchen table, listening to the peas tumble into your bowl.

Makes 4 servings

2 teaspoons unsalted butter

1 cup finely chopped onion

½ pound arugula, washed and
    trimmed

1½ cups cooked peas, fresh
    or previously frozen

2 cups chicken or vegetable broth,
    divided

Kosher salt and freshly ground
    black pepper

Sour cream, thinned with a bit
    of water, to serve

In a large saucepan, melt the butter over medium heat and sauté the onion until tender and translucent, about 8 to 10 minutes. Add the arugula, peas, and 1 cup of the broth and simmer for 1 to 2 minutes, just until the arugula wilts. Let cool slightly.

Puree the vegetables and broth until smooth with a regular or immersion blender. Heat the remaining 1 cup of broth in a saucepan until barely simmering and stir in the pureed vegetables. Simmer for 2 to 3 minutes, but don't let the soup boil. Remove from the heat and season with salt and pepper. Chill until nice and cold. When you're ready to serve the soup, drizzle the sour cream over the top of each bowl.

Chicken and Raspberry Salad with Poppy Seed Dressing

A cooked chicken is one of the most useful things you can keep in your fridge in summertime. Spend a few minutes on a Sunday roasting or poaching it, and then it's at your beck and call all week. Pull off a hunk, put it on a piece of whole grain bread with some leafy greens and a smear of Dijon mustard and it's an instant lunch, or make a Mediterranean platter of homemade sliced chicken paired with store-bought hummus, baba ghanouj, and red pepper spread. But to truly combine refreshment and satisfaction, make a summer chicken salad. Skip the mayo, add tart raspberries, crunchy nuts, and a raspberry poppy seed dressing, and eat in the summer breeze.

Makes 4 servings

FOR THE SALAD

1 (14-ounce) can chicken broth

Kosher salt

2 boneless, skinless chicken breasts

4 cups mixed young greens

½ cup sliced almonds

1 cup raspberries

FOR THE DRESSING

¼ cup raspberries

1 shallot, chopped

2 teaspoons Dijon mustard

¼ cup cider vinegar

2 tablespoons extra-virgin olive oil

½ teaspoon poppy seeds

Kosher salt and freshly ground
   black pepper to taste

In a large saucepan, bring the chicken broth and 3 cups of water to a gentle simmer. Salt the chicken breasts on both sides and add to the broth. Poach gently over medium-low heat, uncovered, for 7 minutes, then remove from the heat, cover tightly, and let the chicken finish cooking in its cooking liquid for 30 minutes to an hour. Remove the chicken from the pot and cut a slit in the center of the chicken breast to check doneness. Dice and chill until you're ready to eat.

To make the dressing, combine all of the dressing ingredients in a blender and puree until smooth. Taste for salt and pepper and adjust if you like. Set aside.

To finish the salad, toss the greens with half of the dressing, then arrange on plates topped with almonds, raspberries, and diced chicken. Drizzle a bit more dressing over the top of the salad.

Vietnamese Summer Rolls with Shrimp, Mint, and Mango

The sun is scorching and the heat is sweltering . . . and there's just one thing to do. Pretend you're languishing in the tropics of Vietnam and make up a batch of shrimp and mango summer rolls. These rolls balance hot, sour, salty, and sweet flavors like all great Southeast Asian food should, and they're even prettier than sushi (but just as low-fat/high-flavor). This forest of vegetables, noodles, and fresh green herbs, wrapped up in tender rice paper makes a great lunch. You can cut them up like maki-type sushi rolls and eat them with chopsticks, or leave them whole and treat them like finger food. The most fastidious Canyon Ranch chef couldn't find anything to object to in these morsels.

Makes 3 to 4 servings

2 ounces glass noodles
   (bean thread noodles)
12 jumbo shrimp, shelled and
   deveined
8 rice paper wrappers
   (6 to 8 inches in diameter)
½ English hothouse cucumber, peeled
   and cut into matchsticks
1 mango, peeled, pitted,
   and cut into matchsticks
6 red leaf lettuce leaves
1 bunch fresh mint
1 bunch fresh cilantro

Soak the noodles in 2 cups of hot water for about 20 minutes, until resilient but tender. Drain and dry with paper towels. Transfer to a bowl and cover.

Cook the shrimp in boiling salted water until pink, about 6 minutes. Drain the shrimp, cut them lengthwise right down the middle, and set aside.

To assemble the rolls, fill a medium bowl with more hot water and spread out a clean dish towel as your work surface. Dip a rice wrapper in the hot water for 30 seconds to a minute, until pliable, then set it on the towel. Arrange two shrimp halves along the bottom third of the wrapper closest to you, along with a small amount of noodles, matchsticks of cucumber and mango, a lettuce leaf, and as much mint and cilantro as you want (I like 6 or 8 sprigs of each).

Fold in the ends of the rice wrapper, and roll up tightly. Transfer to a serving plate and arrange seam-side down. Repeat to make the remaining rolls. They'll get prettier as you go.

Passion Fruit and Vanilla Pavlova

Pavlova is nothing more than a giant crispy vanilla meringue with a marshmallow middle, spread generously with whipped cream and covered with the perfumed, acidic wonder that is passion fruit pulp. It's pretty much irresistible. After all, it's everything you want from a summer dessert—an easy, luscious pedestal for terrific fruit.

If you've never tried passion fruit, I beg you to try this recipe. Track down truly ripe passion fruit. The dark, wrinkled specimens have an unforgettable flavor that's so right in the summer. You can bake the meringue the night before and leave it in the oven until you're ready to put dessert together.

Makes one 7-inch Pavlova

FOR THE MERINGUE

4 large egg whites

1 cup sugar

1 teaspoon white vinegar

½ tablespoon cornstarch

FOR THE TOPPING

1 cup heavy cream

1½ tablespoons sugar

1 teaspoon vanilla extract

8 to 10 ripe, wrinkled passion fruits

Preheat the oven to 250°F. Line a baking sheet with parchment paper and draw a 7-inch circle in the center of the paper as a guide for the shape of the meringue.

In a very clean large bowl, beat the egg whites with an electric mixer until they hold soft peaks. As you continue to beat the whites, gradually add the sugar, and then beat the whites until they hold stiff peaks. To test whether the sugar is fully dissolved, rub a bit of egg white between your fingers. If it still feels gritty, keep beating until the sugar is incorporated. Sprinkle the vinegar and cornstarch over the whites and gently fold in with a rubber spatula.

Spread the meringue mixture evenly within the circle on the parchment paper and transfer the baking sheet to the oven. Bake for 1 hour and 15 minutes, or until the meringue is crisp and ivory-colored. Turn the oven off, leave the oven door slightly ajar, and let the meringue cool completely in the oven.

When you're ready to eat the pavlova, whip the cream to soft peaks with an electric mixer, then add the sugar and vanilla and beat until combined. Peel the parchment paper off the meringue, flip the meringue over, and place on a serving plate. Mound the whipped cream on top of the meringue. Cut the passion fruits in half and scoop the orange pulp straight onto the whipped cream. Slice the pavlova into fat wedges and serve right away.

Mixed Berries in Five-Spice Syrup

Berries are the ideal beauty-day dessert. Simple and beautiful, they're also packed with anti-aging antioxidants. Drizzle them with a spice-infused syrup that brings out the best in even sub par fruit, and you have a dessert that tastes great solo or paired with lemon sorbet.

Makes 3 to 4 servings

1 cinnamon stick, broken

4 cloves

1 star anise

1 (1-inch) piece fresh ginger, peeled

4 black peppercorns

½ cup sugar

3 cups fresh berries (blackberries, blueberries, sliced strawberries, and/or raspberries)

Combine the spices, sugar, and 1 cup of water in a medium saucepan. Bring to a simmer over medium heat and cook, stirring occasionally, until the syrup turns clear and becomes slightly thickened and very aromatic. Let the syrup cool until just slightly warm, about 15 minutes.

Place the berries in a medium bowl and drizzle the cooled syrup over them. Toss gently with your hands, then let the berries macerate until the flavors of the syrup have fully infused the fruit, about 30 minutes.

Inviting Invitations

Invitations: hardly anyone bothers with the real thing anymore, except for weddings and bar mitzvahs. But their rarity makes them even more special when received—especially if they're handmade. Everyone loves getting a pretty envelope with an even prettier invitation inside. Elaborate invites are nice if you have the patience, but you can create just as much impact by staying simple. Here are some ideas for your next get-together.

Form a foundation. For the easiest cards, stick to a single-page (not folded) format—that way, you only have to decorate one page. Paper quality is paramount here. Go for nice, thick card stock from a stationery store, and cut it into rectangles or squares that fit into a nice envelope.

Pick your colors wisely. As for the color of the card stock, consider what kind of mood you want your party to have. If you're throwing a spa party, for instance, and purity and serenity are what you're going for, stick to shades of blue and green. For a luxe feeling, be bold and go with a saturated red. And for an earthy/organic vibe, pick a blond-wood or gentle brown color.

Envelope your invite. A pretty envelope can add that last bit of oomph to any invite. Buy colored envelopes in a contrasting color, or stick to simple white ones and add a flourish of your own.

Use simple text. Printing invitations on your computer is tricky without a special program, so whip out your favorite felt marker or metallic pen and practice your best penmanship. Grouping the lines of text tightly at the top or the bottom of the page leaves room for an accent (see below) and often looks more polished. "Come over for a day of dainty delicacies and sublime spa treatments" would start it off nicely.

Just add beauty. Here's where your invitation gets interesting. Gather patterned paper, colored tissue paper, striking clip-outs from magazines, ribbons, or dried flowers. Devise a simple, signature touch for the invitations. It could be a prim, pretty bow tied to the corner of the invite, or two shades of tissue paper glued to the corners. Whatever you do, try to resist the urge to collage too many different elements together—usually, just one will be more than enough.

Spa Water

One of my best friends once impressed me immensely when I came to her house one summer's day. I asked for something to drink, and she poured me a glass of something divine: cucumber-scented water. They don't say cool as a cucumber for nothing—it was sweet, delicate, and even more refreshing than simple water. She kept pitchers of it in her fridge all summer, and now I do, too. I drink it like a fish when I'm thirsty, and offer it garnished with a cucumber to lucky guests. When I feel like a change, I make tart, ruby-colored hibiscus water, or rustic barley water instead. All three manage to be so much better (and less expensive) than store-bought bottled drinks. Dried hibiscus is sold at Mexican and Jamaican markets, or you can substitute hibiscus-and-rose-hip Pompadour tea, sold in Eastern European markets.

Cucumber Water: Add plenty of slices of English seedless cucumber to a pitcher or glass of water. Let sit for at least 30 minutes for serving.

Hibiscus Water: Bring 4 cups of water to a boil and add ½ cup dried hibiscus, sorrel blossoms, or 4 Pompadour teabags. Let steep for 15 minutes, then strain and add sugar to taste. Chill before serving.

Barley Water: Toast 2 tablespoons of raw, unhulled (whole-grain) barley in a skillet over medium heat, stirring occasionally, until it turns a dark coffee color, about 10 minutes. Meanwhile, heat 4 cups of water in a medium saucepan until boiling. Add the barley to the boiling water and simmer for 10 to 15 minutes. Let cool and chill before serving.

Bliss at Home

Remember, a home spa day should be as relaxing for you as it is for your guests. So resist the urge to go overboard. There's no need to bury your friends in mud in the bathtub or administer volcanic-stone full-body massages. Instead, simply clean your living room and bathroom with loving care, set out items for basic spa treatments, and let each person help herself. Arrange all the supplies on a table over a pretty dishcloth or tray before your guests arrive so there's nothing for you to do but pamper yourself. For an extra special touch, make your own Customizable Face Oil (see page 117).

Here's a checklist—pick and choose the ones you like best.

Prep

AROMATHERAPY CANDLES. Burn your favorite ones while everyone's doing treatments. Skip the candles during eating time.

FLOWERS. A big vase of blooms in your living room and a little bud vase in the bathroom instantly add Zen-like polish to the room and bring smiles to your friends' faces.

TOWELS. A nice big stack of fluffy hand towels and/or washcloths are endlessly useful when pampering. Get cheap extras at a discount department store.

SOCKS. Thin, clean white socks are best for skin-softening foot treatments. Snag a big stack.

TAMED TRESSES. Supply a pile of scrunchies, clips, and/or cloth headbands to manage unruly hair.

Treats

FOOT SCRUBS. A group spa session is the perfect incentive to tackle long-neglected feet. Take turns presoaking feet in a bathtub basin or the bathtub itself (rinse the tub well between each use). Then apply a healthy amount of scrub and massage feet with slow, circular strokes. Rinse off and towel dry, then, for an extra dose of pampering, slather with body lotion and slip on socks. Let the moisturizer work for 15 to 30 minutes, and then remove the socks and gently towel off any excess cream.

FACIAL SCRUB. You just want to lightly buff the skin, not rub it raw, so avoid the extremes—microdermabrasion kits and old-school apricot kernel scrubs are both too harsh to work on all your friends' skins. Instead, go for a gentle scrub that uses synthetic, perfectly round beads or sugar crystals.

The Good, the Bad & the Yummy

FACIAL MASK. Gentle heat transforms an everyday mask into a spa-worthy experience—the warmth opens up your pores and makes the mask even more effective. Transfer a generous amount of mask to a small bowl, stir in a spoonful of water, and microwave for 30-second intervals, stirring well between each, until the mask is warm (but not hot) to the touch.

FACIAL MOISTURIZERS. Instead of supplying your own personal favorite (probably an expensive proposition), have your guests BYOM (Bring-Your-Own-Moisturizer) instead. Picky types can then be certain their skin won't freak out from an unfamiliar brand, and adventurous types can try out new brands.

Customizable Face Oil

Making your own customizable face oil is easy, and in no time, you'll have an all-purpose product that works great as a cleanser, makeup remover, and moisturizer. Mix up the base oil, then pour it into small bowls and let your friends stir together their own customized versions just by adding a few drops of essential oil or honey.

You can buy pure base oils and essential oils from any good health food store or supermarket. If you like, you can even pick up a few small bottles and a tiny funnel so friends can take their personalized oil home with them.

Start out with 2 tablespoons of hazelnut, almond, grapeseed, or rose hip seed oil per person, then have your friends personalize the oil with 30 drops of one of the following essential oils:

FOR DRY SKIN: Rose essential oil

FOR NORMAL SKIN: Lavender essential oil

FOR OILY SKIN: Eucalyptus essential oil

—bad←

SOUTHERN SOUL SHINDIG

Nothing says party quite like a spicy, greasy, mayonnaise-laden shindig. Let other people throw buttoned-up parties with fancy things on sticks and mini-quiches or college-type parties featuring take-out pizza and chips and salsa. Those options might satisfy your guests' hunger, but they don't create the right mood. Instead, strike a balance between simple and fancy and cook up some soul food. The sheer caloric abandon and down-home flavor encourage people to kick back and have a good time. Forget about chopsticks, fancy plates, and cocktail shakers—instead, think mayonnaise, Tabasco, sweet iced tea, and hot fried chicken. Who cares that soul food isn't finger food? It's finger-licking good.

The King's Peanut Butter, Bacon, and Banana Special

Elvis might have been horribly misguided about drugs and sequins, but he got one thing right—peanut butter and banana sandwiches. Cut them into wedges and pile them high.

Makes 16 servings

8 slices bacon

16 slices white sliced sandwich bread

1½ cups peanut butter

4 bananas, thinly sliced

About ¼ pound (1 stick)
  unsalted butter

In a large skillet, fry the bacon until crispy, then drain on paper towels. Cut each piece of bacon in half.

Spread half of the bread slices with an equal amount of peanut butter, then arrange an equal number of banana slices and bacon over the peanut butter on each slice. Top with the remaining bread slices to form sandwiches.

Heat a large nonstick skillet over medium-low heat, and melt 2 teaspoons of butter in the pan. Add two sandwiches to the pan and brown both sides. Repeat with the remaining sandwiches, then cut them into wedges to serve.

Spicy Fried Chicken

Your friends will love you for making them piles of fried chicken—especially when it's been marinated in plenty of buttermilk and Tabasco. This is good piping hot or cold. Marinate the chicken and prepare the batter the night before, then fry the chicken the day of the party.

Makes 12 to 16 servings

Two 3½-pound chickens,
   each cut into 8 pieces

FOR THE MARINADE

7 cups buttermilk

1¼ cups kosher salt

10 garlic cloves, smashed but
   not peeled

⅓ cup Tabasco, or your favorite
   hot sauce

1 tablespoon paprika

3 bay leaves, crushed

FOR THE BATTER

1 large egg

1 teaspoon baking powder

½ teaspoon baking soda

1 cup buttermilk

FOR THE FRYING

4 cups all-purpose flour

A big bottle of canola or peanut oil

Combine the marinade ingredients in a large roasting tray, then add the chicken and let marinate in the fridge for at least 2 to 3 hours and up to a day.

Remove the chicken pieces from the marinade and drain on a rack set over a baking sheet. Whisk the ingredients for the batter together in a medium bowl.

Spread the flour in a large pan. Toss the chicken pieces in the flour to coat, then transfer the chicken to the batter. Let the excess batter drain from the chicken, then gently toss the chicken in the flour once more.

To fry the chicken, heat the oil to 375°F. over medium heat in a cast-iron skillet or large pot (if you don't have a candy thermometer, you can gauge the temperature by dipping a bit of chicken in the oil—it should sizzle and bubble immediately). Add five or six pieces of chicken to the pan, cover, and cook for 7 minutes. Uncover the pan, flip the chicken, and cook *uncovered* for 7 minutes more. Drain the chicken on paper bags (they absorb grease better than paper towels). Serve hot, warm, or cold.

World's Richest Mac and Cheese

The one and only. This version nicely toes the line between the childhood memory of mac and cheese from a box and the gussied-up restaurant versions filled with exotic cheeses. Cabot's makes a reliable cheddar that's perfect for this recipe.

Makes 8 to 10 servings

1 pound dried elbow macaroni

4 cups whole milk

6 tablespoons unsalted butter

6 tablespoons all-purpose flour

1 teaspoon kosher salt

½ teaspoon freshly ground
   black pepper

1 teaspoon Tabasco sauce

½ teaspoon mustard powder

½ pound Gruyère cheese, grated
   (about 2 cups)

¾ pound extra-sharp Cheddar cheese,
   grated (3 cups)

Preheat the oven to 375°F. Butter a 13 x 9-inch baking dish.

Cook the macaroni in plenty of boiling salted water until al dente, about 7 minutes (you'll be cooking it further in the oven).

Meanwhile, in a small saucepan, heat the milk until almost boiling, then set aside. In a large pot, heat the butter until melted, then whisk in the flour and cook for 2 minutes, whisking constantly, until it forms a thick roux. Immediately whisk in the hot milk and cook for 2 to 3 minutes more, until the mixture is thick and smooth.

Remove the sauce from the heat and add the salt, pepper, Tabasco, and mustard powder. Add the cheeses, reserving ½ cup of each for the topping. Whisk the cheese sauce well and adjust the seasonings to taste. Add the cooked macaroni and toss to combine. Transfer the cheesy macaroni to the prepared casserole dish and sprinkle evenly with the reserved cheeses. Bake for 30 to 35 minutes, or until the cheese is nicely browned on top.

Sweet and Sticky BBQ Ribs

Even the daintiest girl can appreciate making a mess of a plate of ribs. So don't shy away from cooking up a batch yourself—you'll soon see, as I did, that it takes just time, not any mysterious skill, to cook up a great batch. Start out with your favorite pre-made BBQ sauce, doctored up with a bit of extra spice and sweetness, and bake the ribs in the morning or the day before the BBQ to give them the time they need to become pull-apart tender.

Makes 8 to 10 servings

3 pounds baby back or spareribs

1 cup barbecue sauce

2 tablespoons unsalted butter, melted

2 tablespoons lemon juice

3 tablespoons mustard or
   mustard powder

Preheat the oven to 350°F. Place the ribs in a large baking pan.

In a medium bowl, whisk together the remaining ingredients and brush all over the ribs.

Bake the ribs, basting them occasionally, for 2 to 2½ hours, or until well browned and fork-tender.

Fresh Corn Cornbread

Moist, barely sweet cornbread is made even better with an extra dose of whole corn kernels adding chewy texture. For a spicier version, stir a can of chopped green chiles into the batter. No one likes a dry batch of cornbread, so take care to bake it just until a toothpick inserted in the center comes out clean.

Makes 16 to 20 servings

½ pound (2 sticks) unsalted
   butter, melted

½ cup honey

4 eggs, beaten

2 cups buttermilk

2 cups cornmeal

2 cups all-purpose flour

2 teaspoons baking powder

½ teaspoon baking soda

1 teaspoon kosher salt

1 cup frozen corn kernels, thawed

Preheat the oven to 375°F. Butter a 13 x 9-inch baking pan.

In a large bowl, whisk the melted butter and honey together until combined. Add the eggs and buttermilk and beat well to combine. In a separate bowl, whisk the cornmeal, flour, baking powder, baking soda, and salt together, and then fold them into the buttermilk mixture, stirring just until combined. Fold in the corn kernels.

Pour the batter into the baking pan and bake for 55 to 60 minutes, or until a toothpick inserted in the center of the cornbread comes out clean.

Crunchy Cabbage-Apple Coleslaw

Cool, crunchy coleslaw is a vital counterpoint to a mouthful of barbecued ribs. If you have leftover ribs or fried chicken after the party, pull the meat off the bone and pile it into a crusty roll along with a big clump of coleslaw. A food processor with the grater disc attachment is the best way to shred the cabbage and apple.

Makes 10 to 12 servings

⅓ cup mayonnaise

1 tablespoon Dijon mustard

1 tablespoon lemon juice

½ teaspoon kosher salt

½ teaspoon freshly ground
    black pepper

1 (16-ounce) package shredded
    coleslaw mix or 6 cups shredded
    cabbage

1 Granny Smith apple,
    peeled and grated

In a large bowl, whisk the mayonnaise, mustard, lemon juice, salt, and pepper together. Add the cabbage and apple and toss to coat in the dressing. Chill for at least an hour before serving.

Banana Icebox Pie

Icebox pies have gone out of fashion, which makes them even cooler than ever. This one, packed with vanilla pudding and bananas, has a creamy, ultra-sugary edge that's just perfect after a spicy soul food dinner. You could, of course, make the vanilla pudding from a mix, but you'll be missing out on discovering just how heavenly the real thing is.

Makes 1 (10-inch) pie

1 (12-ounce) box vanilla wafers

3 ripe bananas

FOR THE VANILLA PUDDING

2 large eggs yolks,
    at room temperature

2 cups whole milk

1 tablespoon all-purpose flour

1/3 cup sugar

2 tablespoons unsalted butter

1/4 teaspoon lemon juice

Pinch of kosher salt

1 teaspoon vanilla extract

Whipped cream, to serve

Preheat the oven to 325°F. Lightly grease a 10-inch pie pan.

Cover the bottom of the pie pan with vanilla wafers. Next, line the sides of the pan with wafers so that the flat side of the wafers are facing the center of the pan. Thinly slice 1½ bananas and layer the slices over the wafers. Repeat layers of wafer and banana, then top with a final layer of wafers. Set the pie dish aside.

Next, make the pudding. In a small bowl, lightly beat the egg yolks and set aside.

In another small bowl, combine ¼ cup of the milk with the flour and stir to make a smooth paste. In a non-aluminum, non-reactive pan, whisk the flour paste with the rest of the milk, sugar, butter, lemon juice, salt, and vanilla.

Cook over medium heat, stirring with a wooden spoon, until the mixture is steaming hot. Remove ½ cup of the hot mixture from the pan and whisk it into the egg yolks. Pour the egg-yolk mixture back into the pan and cook, stirring constantly with a wooden spoon, until mixture boils and thickens, about 15 to 20 minutes. Remove the pudding from the heat and let cool slightly.

Pour the vanilla pudding over the pie plate filled with wafers and bananas. Chill the pie for 4 to 6 hours. When ready to serve, top with dollops of whipped cream.

Hot-Cold Strawberry Shortcake

These are the strawberry shortcakes of my dreams. Hot, salty biscuits collide with sweet, cold vanilla ice cream and juicy strawberries, and the contrast is explosively good. I've been obsessed with them ever since childhood, when my mom used to take me and my sister to Roy Rogers and we'd have them for dessert. No need to make the biscuit dough yourself—just buy pre-made biscuit dough and add extra crunch with an egg wash and a sprinkle of sugar.

Since these treats are all about the temperature differential, put the biscuits in the oven only when you're ready to eat dessert (the sauce can be made up to 4 hours ahead of time). Serve the shortcake in wide bowls, with spoons to catch all of the pink berry and melted vanilla ice cream.

Makes 10 servings

2 pints strawberries, hulled and sliced

⅔ cup plus 2 tablespoons granulated sugar

1 (10-ounce) package biscuit dough (10 biscuits)

1 egg

2 pints vanilla ice cream

In a medium bowl, mash half of the strawberries with ⅔ cup of the sugar until a thick, lumpy sauce forms. Fold the rest of the sliced strawberries into the strawberry sauce and set aside at room temperature.

When you're ready, make the biscuits. Preheat the oven according to the package directions and arrange the biscuits on a cookie sheet. In a small bowl, beat the egg with 2 tablespoons of water and brush onto the tops of the biscuits. Sprinkle the biscuits with the remaining 2 tablespoons of sugar and bake according to the package directions.

Let the biscuits cool for just a couple of minutes, then split each biscuit in half. Lay the bottoms in individual shallow bowls and top with scoops of ice cream and strawberry sauce. Cover with the biscuit tops and serve right away.

HOT CANDY

If you've already decided to indulge in fried chicken, why not go whole hog and deep-fry some candy bars, too? When battered and fried, candy bars are transformed from mere junk food into pure edible luxury. (Deep-fried Mars bars are very popular in the UK, although Snickers and 3 Musketeers bars work equally well!) Bite into a deep-fried candy bar, and the crispy coating reveals a center of melting chocolate and molten nougat that's as sticky and rich as pecan pie. Gather your friends around the stove as you cook them—they'll start out skeptical and shocked, but will soon become converts.

A full-size deep-fried candy bar can be a bit overwhelming, so buy a bag of mini candy bars, or cut each full-size bar in half. Then, for every 10 to 20 small candy bars, mix together 1 cup unbleached all-purpose flour, ½ cup cornstarch, a pinch of baking soda, and a pinch of salt. Whisk in enough beer, seltzer, or water to thin the mixture until it's like pancake batter. Heat at least 2 inches of vegetable oil in a large pot over medium heat until a drop of batter sizzles immediately. Dip each candy bar in the batter and fry until light golden and crisp. Drain on paper towels and devour.

A Little Bit of Soul

Music can make or break a party. But when you're making the food in this chapter, the music is a no-brainer. Soul food needs soul music. Your chicken will taste just a little bit crunchier when you're listening to Al Green, your banana pie just a little bit sweeter.

Dusty in Memphis, Dusty Springfield
The Absolute Best, Al Green
Fresh, Sly and the Family Stone

(The Very Best Of) Curtis Mayfield
Lean On Me, Bill Withers
(The Very Best Of) Kool & the Gang

Jell-O Shots: 2 Kinds

Everybody secretly loves Jell-O shots. They're sweet, they're tasty, and they get you good and sloshed. Plus, they are a godsend to party hosts—instead of investing in liquor and ice, they just mix up the shots in advance and it's all done. But Jell-O shots can be even more delicious—just flavor them Southern-style and they'll fit right in to a soul-food party. These Jell-O shot recipes are inspired by two classic Southern drinks, sweet tea and the mint julep. Serve them in small paper cups for easy enjoyment.

Makes 16 (1-ounce) shots

Sweet Tea Jell-O Shots

2 black tea bags

1 cup boiling water

1 (6-ounce) package Lemon Jell-O

1 cup vodka

In a medium bowl, steep the tea bags in the boiling water for 5 minutes, then remove and discard the bags. Add the Lemon Jell-O and stir to dissolve. Mix in the vodka, and divide the mixture between 16 paper cups. Chill for 3 to 4 hours, or until firm.

Mint Julep Jell-O Shots

1 cup water

1 bunch fresh mint

1 (6-ounce) package Lime Jell-O

1 cup bourbon

In a small saucepan, bring the water to a boil and toss in the mint. Let simmer for 2 minutes, then remove the saucepan from the heat and strain out the mint leaves. Add the Lime Jell-O and stir to dissolve. Mix in the bourbon, and divide the mixture between 16 paper cups. Chill for 3 to 4 hours, or until firm.

CHAPTER 6

Share the Love

From birthdays and holidays, to anniversaries and thank-yous, our days are filled with reasons to give gifts (and drain our wallets). But a gifty occasion is the perfect chance to indulge that D.I.Y. urge, the hankering to craft something with your own two hands.

Of course, you could knit a scarf or paint a watercolor. But a homemade food gift can be just as impressive and isn't nearly as tricky to make. It's hard to predict whether someone will like a CD or a sweater, but everyone likes deliciousness. The only question is whether you want your food gift to say "shameless richness" or "elegant gourmet."

If you want to indulge someone (or a few someones), there's nothing better to do than tie on an apron, pull out the butter, and start some good, old-fashioned baking in the "Bad" section. If you're looking for a lighter and more refined gift, presented with ribbons and bows instead of tinfoil, the recipes in the "Good" section fit the bill. Either way, you'll create a gift so wonderful that you almost want to keep it for yourself.

¿

Go Good or Bad?

A QUICK DIAGNOSTIC QUIZ

if you

find yourself with the baking bug, be **Bad**

want to give food gifts that last, be **Good**

have to bring treats to the office, be **Bad**

know a foodie with a birthday coming up, be **Good**

want to tempt your super-slim friends with empty calories,

be **Bad**

?

good FANCY-PANTS TREATS

No one really knows where we get the D.I.Y. urge—that mysterious force that inspires us to get off the couch and *make* something. Some folks suddenly can't bear to be without their knitting needles. Others dismantle their sofas and build arctic forts. But when the urge strikes, hardly anyone thinks of making food. Food gifts, that is. An edible gift can be as gorgeous as a hand-knit angora sweater, and a whole lot more enjoyable in the mouth. They're almost universally appealing—hardly anyone is capable of refusing a box of choco-late-dipped figs—and you can indulge your urge to embellish by packaging and wrapping it with a careful eye.

Just like any craft project, food gifts beg to be personalized. A lovingly packaged gift is a great way to show off your thoughtfulness and style. Scour stationery shops and flea mar-kets for the perfect ribbons and boxes. Devise your own color schemes and design your own tags. And be sure to check out the headnote of each recipe for any recipe variations that strike your fancy. Homemade gifts are especially perfect for Christmas. When everyone else is indulging in rampant consumerism and spending gobs of money, you can avoid the crowds and make gifts that have that rare homemade touch. And that's love in a nutshell.

Strawberry Basil Jam

Most people are afraid of making jam. The big secret is that it's really not hard at all. After all, you're just cooking fruit with some sugar and putting it in a jar. The plus side to jam's difficult reputation is that people will be inordinately impressed when you present them with a homemade jar of the stuff. For the very berriest strawberry jam, track down the best fruit you can find (local, farmer's market fruit is ideal) but don't be a purist about it. Even jam made in the winter with fruit from Mexico is better than most versions you can buy at the store—especially if you finish the jam with a bit of fresh basil. Only a couple of extra items are needed: five jam jars (track them down in the baking aisle of the supermarket or go to a kitchen-supply store) and a candy thermometer. If you want to double or halve the recipe, feel free. The jam will keep for about two months in the refrigerator.

Jam is always best with fruit that's plentiful and in season—it's also cheapest that way, too. So if strawberries aren't at their peak when you're ready to put up a few jars, feel free to substitute other berries, and another herb for the basil. Blueberries and blackberries are delicious with a few sprigs of fresh thyme and raspberries work well with lavender.

Makes 8 (½-pint) jars

6 pounds whole ripe strawberries, trimmed

¼ cup freshly squeezed lemon juice

3 cups sugar

5 whole fresh basil leaves

Wash your jam jars and lids with soap and water, and dry them thoroughly. Line a baking sheet with parchment paper or aluminum foil and arrange the jars and lids on top (the lids should be alongside, not on, the jars). Set the baking sheet aside and preheat the oven to 220°F. When the jam is 5 minutes from being done, sterilize the jars by putting the baking sheet with the empty jars in the hot oven for 5 minutes.

Place the strawberries and lemon juice in a large pot and cook over low heat, stirring occasionally, for about 40 minutes, or until plenty of juices are released. Add the sugar and basil and increase the heat to medium. Continue cooking, stirring occasionally, until the jam registers 210°F. on a candy thermometer, about 15 minutes.

Ladle the hot jam into the sterilized jars on the lined baking sheet (the parchment paper will catch any spills), carefully screw on the tops, and set them upside-down until they come to room temperature. Tighten the lids before storing in the fridge.

Apricot Thyme Chutney

This is a tart, sweet, and not-too-spicy chutney with a gorgeous orange color and a surprising range of uses. Spread it on chicken pieces before baking them, and it forms a delectable sweet glaze. Combine with a small can of tomatoes and use as a sweet-and-sour sauce for meatballs. Or simply smear the chutney on a turkey sandwich or use as a topping for vanilla ice cream. Best of all, the recipes calls for dried, not fresh, apricots, so you can make this year-round. You'll need four jam jars (available in the baking aisle at many supermarkets, or in a kitchen-supply store) and a candy thermometer. The chutney will keep for about 2 to 3 months in the fridge.

Makes 10 (½-pint) jars

¼ cup extra-virgin olive oil

2 large onions, thinly sliced

2 garlic cloves, minced

2 tablespoons minced fresh ginger

2 jalapeño pepper,
  seeded and finely chopped

2 tablespoons minced fresh thyme

4 cups dried apricots, soaked in hot
  water for 30 minutes, drained, then
  coarsely chopped

¼ cup packed light brown sugar

2 cups apple cider vinegar

½ cup coarsely chopped fresh cilantro

Kosher salt and freshly ground black
  pepper, to taste

Wash your jam jars and lids with soap and water, and dry them thoroughly. Line a baking sheet with parchment paper or aluminum foil and arrange the jars and lids on top (the lids should be alongside, not on, the jars). Set the baking sheet aside and preheat the oven to 220°F. When the chutney is 5 minutes from being done, sterilize the jars by putting the baking sheet with the empty jars in the hot oven for 5 minutes.

To make the chutney, heat the oil in a large pot over medium-high heat. Add the onions and cook until soft and lightly golden, stirring occasionally, about 20 to 25 minutes. Stir in the garlic, ginger, jalapeño and thyme and cook for 2 minutes more. Add the apricots, brown sugar, and cider vinegar and bring to a boil.

Turn down the heat to medium and simmer the chutney for 30 minutes, stirring occasionally until the chutney registers 210°F. on a candy thermometer, about 25 minutes. Add cilantro and simmer for a few minutes more, then remove the chutney from the heat and season with salt and pepper to taste.

Ladle the hot chutney into the sterilized jam jars on the lined baking sheet (the parchment paper will catch any spills), screw on the tops, and store them upside-down until they come to room temperature.

Masala Spice Mix

If your spice cupboard were bare except for this miraculous mixture of whole spices (cinnamon, star anise, black peppercorns, cloves, and cardamom), you'd still be able to pull off some great meals. Left whole and infused in milk and tea, it makes terrific chai. Ground up and mixed with some olive oil, it transforms into an exotic rub for chicken or fish and adds the perfect layer of nuance to mashed sweet potatoes. Or grind up a couple teaspoons and stir into plain cake batter to make an addictive spice cake. Attach a tag to the jar to explain the masala's many uses. Track down big bags of cheap spices at ethnic markets.

Makes 5 (½-pint) jars

16 cinnamon sticks, broken with a
    mallet or heavy pot into big shards
½ cup cardamom pods, split open
½ cup black peppercorns
½ cup cloves
16 pieces star anise

Layer all the ingredients equally in the glass jars.

Spread the Love

Show off your jams, chutneys, and spice mixtures to maximum effect by packaging them with love and care. Buy adhesive labels from a craft or office supply store and label and date each jar in your best handwriting. Decorate your jars by gluing a round piece of your favorite vintage cloth onto each lid, or tie a broad ribbon that runs from the bottom to the top of each jar. For elegant but rustic packaging, wrap the jars in butcher paper and secure with twine and a single perfect flower (fresh or fake). Take your jars to an even lovelier level by boxing them beautifully.

Bread and Butter Pickles

Homemade pickles sound complicated, but making them is a simple matter of simmering soaked cucumber slices with vinegar and a few spices. Your reward? Pickles that add tang to any dish and never fail to impress. These pickles have freshness and a bright snap that puts any supermarket version to shame. You'll need four pint jars (available in the baking aisle at many supermarkets, or in a kitchen-supply store). These pickles keep for at least a month in the refrigerator.

Makes enough to fill 4 pint jars

3 pounds Kirby cucumbers,
  washed and thinly sliced

½ cup kosher salt

1½ cups white vinegar

1 cup granulated sugar

1 teaspoon ground turmeric

2 teaspoons mustard seeds

1 teaspoon dill seeds

1 teaspoon black peppercorns

10 garlic cloves, peeled

½ cup thinly sliced yellow onions

Place the cucumber slices in a large bowl and sprinkle them with the salt. Add ice and cold water to cover, and let sit for about 6 hours. Drain well.

Sterilize the four pint jars according to the manufacturer's directions.

In a large non-aluminum pot, combine the vinegar, sugar, turmeric, mustard seeds, dill seeds, peppercorns, and garlic with ½ cup of water and place over high heat; boil the mixture for 5 minutes. Add the cucumbers and onions and simmer for 2 minutes. Let the cucumbers cool for 20 minutes.

Divide the pickles between the four hot sterilized jars, leaving about ½ inch of space at the top. Fill a large pot with enough water to come halfway up the sides of the jars. Bring the water to a boil, add the jars, lower the heat slightly, and process the jars at a lively simmer for 15 minutes. Carefully remove the jars from the water with tongs and place on a towel to cool. The pickles should rest in the fridge for about 2 weeks before you eat them, but you can give them as gifts right away!

Chocolate Rounds with Nuts and Dried Cherries

The French call these simple but elegant treats mendiants—I call them my go-to gift for any choco-holic. Simply melt good chocolate in the microwave, drop it by the spoonful on wax paper, sprinkle on pistachios, slivered almonds, and bits of dried cherry, and you're done. Package them in a small, pretty box between layers of wax paper.

Makes 50 candies

11 ounces bittersweet chocolate, chopped

½ cup slivered almonds

½ cup chopped unsalted pistachios, husks rubbed off

⅔ cup dried cherries, roughly chopped

Place the chocolate in a large Pyrex or glass bowl and microwave on high for 30-second intervals, stirring between each round of microwaving. Once almost all of the chocolate is melted, simply whisk the chocolate to melt the rest. The chocolate should feel warm, not hot.

While the chocolate is melting, cover a baking sheet with wax or parchment paper and place the almonds, pistachios, and cherries in separate bowls.

As the chocolate cools and solidifies along the edges, scrape and stir the hardened chocolate back into the melted chocolate with a whisk—this will temper the chocolate and help it become shiny when it solidifies. Continue doing this for about 6 or 7 minutes.

Using a tablespoon, drop dollops of chocolate onto the baking sheet and spread them with the back of the spoon so they become 1½-inch circles. After you've made the first dozen, top them with nuts and cherries and repeat until you've used up all the chocolate and toppings (if you wait until you make all 50 mendiants, the chocolate might become too hard to adhere to the toppings).

Allow the mendiants to harden before packing them.

Chocolate-Dipped Figs

When figs are fresh and ripe, there's nothing to rival them for beauty and deliciousness. Dried figs usually can't hold a candle to them. But when dried figs are plumped up in a lemony syrup and dipped in dark chocolate, they're so good they make fresh figs jealous. These figs need to rest overnight after dipping.

Makes 30 figs

30 plump dried figs (plump
   Calimyrna figs are the best)

1½ cups water

1½ cups sugar

3 strips lemon peel

Juice of 2 lemons

12 ounces bittersweet or
   semisweet chocolate, chopped

First, reshape the figs. Using your hands, gently squeeze the figs until their stems point straight up and they look pretty. Using a skewer or toothpick, poke 2 or 3 small holes in each fig and set aside.

Stir the water, sugar, lemon peel, and lemon juice together in a small saucepan and bring to a simmer, stirring occasionally. Once the sugar is completely dissolved, place the figs in a single layer at the bottom of a large saucepan and simmer for 15 minutes

Remove the figs from the lemon syrup and set them on a rack to drain (resist the urge to drain them on paper towels, since they'll stick). Set up a cookie sheet lined with wax paper.

In a double boiler over simmering water, melt the chocolate, stirring frequently, then remove the double boiler from the heat. Pick up each fig by the stem, dip in the melted chocolate, and place on the cookie sheet to harden.

Let the figs sit out overnight before you pack them up.

Say it with Cellophane

Lovely snacks like chocolate-dipped figs and pastel-colored macaroons are just too pretty to be hidden away in a box. Be an exhibitionist and pack them in see-through cellophane bags instead. The thicker the cellophane, the nicer it looks, so track down quality cellophane bags at stationery or craft stores. Try to get the kind with the square-shaped bottom so the bag can stand upright to neatly hold the sweets. A little square tag with a few sweet words is a nice touch—punch a hole through it and tie it onto the bag with a length of thin ribbon or twine.

Pre-Packaged Happiness

A homemade food gift makes an undeniably impressive present, but to truly maximize its impact, don't simply hand it over to the lucky recipient. Instead, nestle the gift in a truly lovely box to give it the extra bit of polish. You can certainly go to a stationery store and spend a fortune on boxes, wrapping paper, and ribbons, but it's even more charming to channel your inner kindergartener and turn wrapping your present into an art project.

Track down shoe boxes, hatboxes, or other boxes lying around the house and decorate them to your heart's desire. Get a pad of construction paper, cut out abstract, Matisse-like shapes, and glue them on. Use scissors to cut out interesting images from magazines (fashion and nature magazines work especially well). Or cover the boxes with black paper and draw simple designs on the box with a silver pen.

A simple adornment can sometimes make the most impact. You can paint your box blue and top it with a simple red origami crane or a fresh or dried flower. For winter, decorate with snowflakes cut from white paper, or glue tiny flowers like baby's breath along the top edge of the box or wherever else you fancy.

A tag is always a nice touch—use stiff paper in a matching or contrasting color. If the gift you're giving has several different uses, include a short note inside the box with ideas and suggestions.

—bad⇄

EASY-BAKE TREATS

Let's make no bones about it—baking is bad. It's everything the diet dictocrats declare we should ban from our kitchens—refined flour, butter, cream, and white sugar.

And that's why it's so good. It's sugar-rush satisfaction coupled with the comfort of carbs. Now, many women satisfy the craving for desserts by sneaking a chocolate croissant from the bakery or splitting a dainty dessert at a restaurant. But neither of these options satisfies like a good, old-fashioned at-home baking session. The whir of beaters and the licking of the bowl. The divine smells coming out of your very own oven. The masochistic challenge of a tricky recipe. And, finally, a rack of sweet delights that you can share or hoard as you see fit.

In the mood for chocolate? It's here. Need something tart or fruity? That's here, too. No fussy multi-layers, no intimidating techniques. Just baking that's almost as easy as using an Easy-Bake oven.

Lime Curd Thumbprints

There's nothing like a simple, innocent cookie with a sweet-tart center. Luscious lime curd comes together in a snap. You'll have about a cup of extra curd—keep it for yourself to spread on toast in the morning, or tuck it into a small jar and present it to a lucky friend alongside the cookies.

Makes about 40 cookies

FOR THE LIME CURD

6 tablespoons unsalted butter,
  at room temperature

1 cup sugar

2 large egg yolks

2 large eggs

⅔ cup fresh lime juice

1 teaspoon grated lime zest

FOR THE COOKIES

½ pound (2 sticks) unsalted
  butter, at room temperature

½ cup sugar

2 large egg yolks

1 tablespoon lime juice

1 tablespoon grated lime zest

¼ teaspoon kosher salt

2½ cups all-purpose flour

First, make the lime curd. In a large bowl, use an electric mixer to beat the butter with the sugar until well blended. Gradually blend in the egg yolks and eggs. Beat for a minute more, then beat in the lime juice (the mixture will look lumpy, but it will become smooth as it cooks).

Pour the lime mixture into a medium saucepan and set over medium heat, whisking constantly, until the mixture suddenly becomes much thicker, about 10 to 15 minutes. Be sure not to let the lime curd boil.

Pour the lime curd into a clean bowl and stir in the lime zest. Cover the surface of the curd with plastic wrap and chill for at least an hour.

Meanwhile, make the cookies. Preheat the oven to 350°F. Grease a cookie sheet or line it with parchment paper.

Using an electric mixer, cream the butter and sugar together until light and fluffy. Add the egg yolks one by one, beating after each addition, and then beat in the lime juice, zest, and salt. Fold the flour into the butter-egg mixture.

Roll tablespoonfuls of dough into balls and place them on the cookie sheet, leaving 1 inch of space between each cookie. Press your thumb into the center of each ball to create a deep indentation. Fill the cookie centers with a small dollop of lime curd and bake them for 15 to 20 minutes, or until the cookies are light golden. Place the cookie sheet on a rack and let cool for 30 minutes, then remove the cookies and let them cool completely.

Melted Choco-Peanut Butter Sandwiches

These are cookies no certifiable chocoholic will be able to resist. Dark and glittering with sugar on the outside, chewy within, these cookies are sandwiched around a peanut butter and marshmallow filling that sets off the chocolate beautifully. The cookies are also amazing with balls of vanilla ice cream squeezed between them.

Makes 16 cookie sandwiches

2¾ cups all-purpose flour

1 teaspoon baking soda

1 teaspoon baking powder

¼ cup unsweetened Dutch-process
   cocoa powder

½ teaspoon kosher salt

¼ pound plus 4 tablespoons
   (1½ sticks) unsalted butter, divided

¾ cup sugar

2 extra large eggs

2 teaspoons vanilla extract

FOR THE

MARSHMALLOW-PEANUT CREAM

2 cups Marshmallow Fluff

1 cup peanut butter

Preheat the oven to 375°F. Grease a large cookie sheet or line with parchment. Sift the flour, baking soda, baking powder, cocoa powder, and salt together into a large bowl. Set aside.

In a small saucepan, melt 4 tablespoons of the butter over medium-low heat, stirring constantly, until it smells nutty and turns a light golden-brown color, about 5 minutes. Transfer the brown butter to a small bowl to cool.

In a large bowl, use an electric mixer to blend the remaining ¼ pound of butter with the cooled brown butter until light and fluffy. Add the sugar and blend until smooth. Add the eggs one at a time, beating until each egg is thoroughly incorporated. Beat in the vanilla extract.

Turn the mixer speed down to low and add the flour mixture in thirds, beating each addition only just until incorporated. Spoon 32 heaping balls of dough onto the prepared cookie sheet, about 1 inch apart.

Bake for 30 to 35 minutes, or until the cookies are a shiny dark brown and smell very chocolatey. Place the cookie sheet on a rack to cool for 5 minutes, and then transfer the cookies to a rack to cool completely.

While the cookies cool, make the peanut-marshmallow filling. In a medium bowl, beat the Marshmallow Fluff and peanut butter together with an electric mixer until smooth and fluffy. When the cookies are completely cool, spread a generous dose over the flat side of half of the cookies, then sandwich the remaining cookies over the tops.

Banana Walnut Mini-Cakes

This is plain-Jane banana bread, reinvented. These cakes have a sweetness that's balanced by cream cheese frosting, so they work for breakfast, dessert, or random cravings in between. The riper (and blacker) the bananas, the more perfumed the cakes will be. You can use a cupcake pan for this recipe, but for maximum cuteness, try to track down an 8-count mini loaf pan—you'll need to increase the baking time by 5 to 10 minutes.

Makes 12 cupcakes or 8 mini loaf cakes

FOR THE BANANA CAKES

2 cups all-purpose flour

½ teaspoon kosher salt

1 teaspoon baking powder

1 teaspoon ground cinnamon

¼ teaspoon ground nutmeg

¼ pound (1 stick) unsalted butter, at room temperature

½ cup granulated sugar

½ cup light brown sugar, packed

2 large eggs

½ cup sour cream

1 cup mashed ripe or over-ripe bananas (2 bananas)

¾ cup walnuts, roughly chopped

FOR THE CREAM CHEESE FROSTING

1 (8-ounce) package cream cheese, at room temperature

2 tablespoons unsalted butter, at room temperature

¾ cup confectioners' sugar

½ teaspoon vanilla extract

1 teaspoon sour cream

Preheat the oven to 350°F. Butter 12 muffin or 8 mini loaf cups.

In a large bowl, sift the flour, salt, baking powder, cinnamon, and nutmeg together. Set aside.

In another large bowl, use an electric mixer to cream the butter, granulated sugar, and brown sugar together until smooth and creamy. Add the eggs one at a time, beating well after each addition. Add the sour cream and mashed bananas and beat until smooth. Fold the flour mixture in just until incorporated, then fold in the walnuts.

Divide the batter between the prepared muffin or mini-loaf cups and bake for 15 to 20 minutes, or until a toothpick inserted in the center comes out clean. Let the pan cool on a wire rack for 15 minutes, and then remove the cakes from the pan and let cool completely.

While the banana cakes are baking, make the frosting. In a medium bowl, use an electric mixer on medium speed to cream the cream cheese and butter together until smooth. Reduce the speed to low and gradually beat in the confectioners' sugar. Add the vanilla and sour cream and beat until smooth.

Spread the cream cheese frosting on the banana cakes.

Sea-Salt Blondies with Dried Cherries and Pecans

Some might suppose that blondies (ahem) pale in comparison to brownies, but nothing could be further from the truth. They just need a little clever accessorizing. Add dried cherries for tartness and color, and a touch of sea salt for nuance, and they'll be divine enough for your most discerning customers.

Makes 8 to 12 servings

¾ cup pecan halves

¼ pound (1 stick) unsalted butter

1½ cups packed dark brown sugar

1 teaspoon sea salt

1 large egg plus 1 large egg yolk, at room temperature

1½ teaspoons vanilla extract

1 cup plus 2 tablespoons all-purpose flour

¾ cup dried cherries

Preheat the oven to 350°F. Butter an 8-inch square baking pan and line the bottom of the pan with parchment or waxed paper. Butter the paper well. Toast the pecans on a baking sheet in the oven for 5 to 10 minutes, stirring once or twice, until lightly toasted. Let the pecans cool a bit, then coarsely chop and set aside.

In a medium saucepan over medium heat, heat the butter, brown sugar, and sea salt, stirring frequently, until the sugar and salt have dissolved. Cook, stirring, about 1 minute longer. Set the pan aside to cool for about 10 minutes.

With a wide spoon or a big fork, stir the egg, egg yolk, and vanilla into the saucepan with the cooled sugar mixture. Add the flour, chopped cherries, and pecans, stirring just until blended.

Pour the batter into the prepared pan and bake until the center is springy when touched and a toothpick inserted in the center comes out clean or just slightly crumby, about 30 to 35 minutes. Set the pan on a rack to cool, then run a table knife around the edge of the blondie and invert it onto a flat serving plate. Peel off the parchment paper and invert again onto the rack to cool completely. Slice into bars before serving.

Raspberry-Stuffed Chocolate Cupcakes

There's no sexier dessert than a cupcake. They're cute, they're girly, and they're flat-out luscious. Stuff them with raspberries and creamy mascarpone cheese and they're downright naughty. Take a few into the bedroom and enjoy.

Makes 12 cupcakes

FOR THE CUPCAKES

2 cups all-purpose flour

1 teaspoon baking soda

¼ teaspoon kosher salt

6 ounces unsweetened chocolate, chopped

½ pound (2 sticks) unsalted butter, softened

1 cup granulated sugar

1 cup firmly packed light brown sugar

4 large eggs, at room temperature

1 teaspoon vanilla extract

1 cup buttermilk

FOR THE FILLING

1¼ cups heavy cream

½ cup confectioners' sugar

1 teaspoon vanilla extract

1 pound mascarpone, at room temperature

¾ cup raspberries, chopped

Whole raspberries, for garnish

Grease a 12-cup muffin tin, or line the cups with cupcake liners. Preheat the oven to 350°F.

Sift the flour, baking soda, and salt together, then set aside. Melt the chocolate in a double boiler over gently simmering water, stirring occasionally. Set the melted chocolate aside, too.

In a large bowl, use an electric mixer on a medium speed to cream the butter until smooth. Add the granulated and brown sugars and continue beating until creamy and fluffy, about 3 minutes. Beat the eggs in one at a time, beating well after each addition. Beat in the melted chocolate until thoroughly blended.

Add the vanilla extract to the cup of buttermilk.

Add the sifted dry ingredients and the buttermilk to the batter in thirds, alternating between the two. Be sure to beat just until the additions disappear into the batter—overbeating makes a tough cake.

Fill the cupcake liners almost three-quarters full with batter and bake for 20 to 25 minutes, or until a toothpick inserted in the center of the cupcake comes out clean.

When the cupcakes have cooled completely, carve a neat hole into the top of each cupcake with a small knife.

To make the raspberry-mascarpone cream, place the cream, confectioners' sugar, vanilla, and mascarpone in a large bowl and beat with an electric mixer on high speed until smooth and fluffy, about 2 minutes. Fold in the chopped raspberries, and transfer the filling to a piping bag with a wide tip (about ½-inch wide). Pipe the cream into the center of each cupcake and top with a whole raspberry.

Brown-Butter Berry Buckle

A buckle is nothing more than buttery dough with a pile of fruit baked on top of it. As the buckle bakes, the dough rises up above the fruit in peaks and valleys. This version has a crust flavored with butter that's been heated until light brown, which adds an almost hazelnutty touch. This is a dessert that everyone attacks with a big serving spoon, digging up dollops of melted fruit and crust until there's nothing left but a puddle of berry juice.

Makes 1 (13-inch) casserole or 1 (13 x 9-inch) cake

FOR THE FRUIT
¼ cup sugar

½ teaspoon ground cinnamon

¼ teaspoon ground nutmeg

6 cups mixed blueberries, blackberries, raspberries, and/or sliced strawberries

Juice of ½ lemon

2 tablespoons cornstarch

¼ cup water

FOR THE BUCKLE
¼ pound (1 stick) unsalted butter

¾ cup unbleached all-purpose flour

2 teaspoons baking powder

1 cup granulated sugar

¾ cup whole milk

Preheat the oven to 350°F. Grease a 13-inch oval casserole dish or a 13 x 9-inch baking dish.

In a large bowl, whisk together the sugar, cinnamon, and nutmeg. Add the berries and toss gently. In a separate small bowl, whisk together the lemon juice, cornstarch, and water, then add the cornstarch mixture to the fruit and toss again. Set the fruit aside.

In a small saucepan, heat the butter over medium-low heat, stirring constantly, until the butter turns a very light tan and smells like toasted hazelnuts. Immediately pour the butter into a small bowl, scraping in any milk solids that cling to the saucepan.

In a separate large bowl, whisk together the flour, baking powder, and sugar, then gradually whisk in the milk. Pour in the brown butter and gently fold it in—don't worry about fully incorporating it into the batter.

Scrape the buckle dough into the prepared pan and scatter the berry mixture (and any juices) evenly over the top. Resist the urge to mix everything together. Bake the buckle for 30 to 35 minutes, or until a toothpick inserted into the buckle emerges with only a few moist crumbs clinging to it. Serve warm or at room temperature.

Chocolate Cognac Bread Pudding

Bread pudding is a homey dessert, but that doesn't mean it needs to be nursery-school sweet. This one's all grown up. Most kids will hate this bread pudding—most adults will love it. Cubes of baguette are tossed with a bittersweet chocolate batter with a dose of cognac to add edge. Be sure to heat it up in a low oven or microwave before serving so it gets cozy and warm, and keep a pint of heavy cream in the fridge for drizzling over the top.

Makes 6 to 8 servings

1 (12-inch) piece day-old baguette, cut into ⅓-inch slices, then slices halved crosswise (4 cups)

3 cups half-and-half

½ cup granulated sugar

⅛ teaspoon kosher salt

10 ounces good-quality bittersweet chocolate, chopped

6 large eggs

1 teaspoon vanilla extract

3 tablespoons cognac

2 tablespoons unsalted butter, cut into small cubes

Chilled heavy cream, to serve

Generously butter a 2 ½- to 3-quart round casserole dish. Place the baguette cubes in the dish.

In a medium saucepan over medium heat, combine the half-and-half, sugar, and salt and cook, stirring, until the sugar dissolves and the mixture is hot but not boiling. Take the saucepan off the heat, add the chocolate, and let stand for 2 minutes. Whisk the mixture until smooth and glossy.

In a large bowl, lightly whisk the eggs, and then, while whisking constantly, gradually add the creamy chocolate mixture. Whisk in the vanilla and cognac. Pour the mixture over the bread cubes in the casserole dish, cover the dish with plastic wrap, and let the bread soak up the chocolate cream for 1 hour at room temperature.

When the bread pudding is ready to bake, preheat the oven to 325°F. Prepare a hot water bath by placing a 13 x 9-inch baking pan in the middle rack of the oven, and then carefully filling it halfway with boiling water. Dot the top of the bread pudding with the cubed butter, then place the casserole dish in the middle of the water-filled baking pan. Bake until the edge of the bread pudding is set but the center is slightly jiggly, about 45 minutes to 1 hour. Remove the casserole dish from the hot water bath and transfer to a rack to cool. Serve warm or slightly reheated, with a thin drizzle of cream.

Pineapple Coconut Upside-Down Cake

Tarte Tatin, or upside-down cake, is a brilliant idea that was reportedly born when a baker put apples on the bottom, rather than the top, of a baking pan filled with cake batter. When the cake is flipped over after baking, the fruit becomes a caramelized and juicy topping. Here, a simple vanilla cake gets a tropical edge from grated coconut, and sunny pineapple replaces the apples. Resist the urge to wait to unmold the cake—it has to be unmolded while it's still warm from the oven or the cake will stick in the pan.

Makes 1 (8-inch) square cake

FOR THE TOPPING

¾ cup packed dark brown sugar

4 tablespoons (½ stick) unsalted butter

1 small ripe pineapple, trimmed, quartered, cored, and cut into ¼-inch-thick slices

FOR THE CAKE

2 cups cake flour

2½ teaspoons baking powder

¼ teaspoon kosher salt

¼ pound (1 stick) unsalted butter, at room temperature

½ cup granulated sugar

2 large eggs

1 teaspoon vanilla extract

½ cup grated coconut

⅔ cup sour cream

Preheat the oven to 350°F. Butter the sides (but not the bottom) of an 8-inch square baking pan.

To make the topping, combine the brown sugar and butter in a small saucepan and cook over medium heat, stirring constantly, until the mixture is smooth and comes to a boil. Pour the caramel into the baking pan and spread evenly over the bottom with a spatula. Layer the pineapple slices evenly over the top, overlapping them a bit, and press the fruit into the caramel. Set the pan aside.

To make the cake batter, sift the flour, baking powder, and salt into a medium bowl. Set aside. In a large bowl, use an electric mixer to beat the butter until smooth. Gradually beat in the sugar and continue beating until fluffy. Add the eggs one at a time, beating well to incorporate each addition. Beat in the vanilla and coconut.

Sprinkle half of the flour mixture over the butter-coconut mixture and, on low speed, mix just until the flour disappears. Add the sour cream and mix until just blended. Gently mix in the remaining flour. Scoop large spoonfuls of batter onto the pineapple in the pan and gently spread it evenly with a table knife. Add the remaining batter. Lightly tap the pan on the counter to settle the batter.

Bake until the cake is golden brown and a toothpick inserted in the center comes out clean, about 45 minutes.

Immediately run a table knife around the edge of the cake, then invert the cake onto a flat serving plate. Let the pan sit upside-down for about 5 minutes before removing it so the pineapple topping can settle. Remove the pan carefully, and replace any fruit topping on the top of the cake.

Red Velvet Chocolate Chip Loaf

Rich with buttermilk and packed with chocolate chips, this treat is as dense as pound cake but even more dastardly. The retro red color only adds to its innate appeal.

Makes 1 large loaf cake

¼ pound plus 4 tablespoons
  (1½ sticks) unsalted butter,
  at room temperature
2½ cups granulated sugar
6 large eggs
1½ teaspoons vanilla extract
1 ounce (1 bottle) red food coloring
3 cups cake flour
¼ teaspoon kosher salt
1 tablespoon cocoa powder
1 teaspoon baking soda
1 tablespoon white vinegar
1 cup buttermilk
1 cup semisweet chocolate chips

Butter and flour a loaf pan and set aside. Preheat the oven to 350°F.

In a large bowl, use an electric mixer to cream the butter until fluffy. Add the sugar and beat until well blended. Beat in the eggs one at a time, then beat in the vanilla extract and food coloring.

In a separate bowl, sift the flour, salt, and cocoa powder together. In a small bowl, dissolve the baking soda in the vinegar, then add the buttermilk and stir to combine.

Fold the flour mixture and the buttermilk alternately into the butter mixture. Fold in the chocolate chips, and pour the batter into the loaf pan.

Bake for 60 to 65 minutes, or until a toothpick inserted in the center of the loaf comes out clean. Let the cake cool in the pan for about 10 minutes, then invert onto a wire rack to cool completely. Cut in thick slices to serve.

Drinkable Desserts

Sure, you can bake chocolate into brownies, cookies, and cakes, but for the most potent, soothing chocolate experience, do what the ancient Aztecs and modern Parisians do—drink it.

For a classic, French-style hot chocolate, mix 4 teaspoons of good-quality cocoa powder (unsweetened) with 1 tablespoon each of sugar and milk in a small saucepan. Add a cup of milk, stir well, and heat until just steaming, then pour into a mug or a dainty teacup. For a delicately spicy hot chocolate, try the Aztec variation—add a pinch of nutmeg and cayenne to the cocoa powder mixture, and stir your exotic hot chocolate with a cinnamon stick.

Snack Cake Nostalgia

Sometimes, all it takes to bring comfort to a troubled soul is a taste of childhood. For most of us, childhood inevitably revolved around a fondness for little snack cakes. The rustle of the plastic wrapping, the way the frosting always stuck to the wrapper (the better to lick it off, my dear) and the familiar taste will bring you back to the happiest sugar-drenched moments of childhood.

Since I grew up in Philadelphia, I was a slave (and still am) to snacks from a cult regional brand called Tastykake, bouncing from chocolate-frosted chocolate cupcakes to butterscotch Krimpets. But even Yodels, Ho Hos, or Twinkies can take you back to a time of innocent, guiltless enjoyment—the perfect antidote to self-conscious, stressed-out adulthood. Here's what your favorite snack cake says about you:

TWINKIES: Sensitive and vulnerable, you crave tenderness and security

YODELS: You long for chaos and a whirlwind of activity

PEANUT BUTTER SANDWICHES: You manage to balance kindness with practicality—bravo!

CUPCAKES: Your conventional nature makes you cautious and a bit predictable

SNO BALLS: Frivolous and artificial, with a taste for extremes, you might just be insane

FRUIT PIES: Behind a tough exterior, you hide a sweet and gooey heart that's ready to break free

Cookie Comfort

Biting into a baked treat can be comforting, but sometimes, the act of baking just isn't—some recipes are just too exhausting for everyday. My advice? If you want to enjoy the process of baking as much as the end result, make sugar cookies. The dough is easy to put together, and decorating the cookies will bring you straight back to the glory days of third grade. Back to days when we learned how to shape dough by playing with Play-Doh, learned how to eat treats by watching Cookie Monster, and learned how to lust after them by selling Girl Scout Cookies. And, if you use fresh ingredients, a sugar cookie rivals a soufflé for sheer deliciousness.

Spread some white frosting on top of each cookie, and it becomes a magnet for the cutest sprinkles, dragees, and tiny candies you can find. You can even create your own personalized, scented sugars to dust on top of the cookies before they bake.

Make flower-scented sugar by pureeing a half cup of sugar with a tablespoon of edible dried flowers like rose or lavender. Freeze-dried fruits like mango, raspberry, and apple make terrific flavored sugars, too—just blend equal parts sugar and freeze-dried fruit. Pretty as a picture, and as easy as pie.

Easy, Pretty Sugar Cookies

Makes about 4 dozen 2-inch cookies

½ pound (2 sticks) unsalted butter, softened

1½ cups granulated sugar

1½ teaspoons baking powder

½ teaspoon kosher salt

1 teaspoon vanilla extract

1 large egg

2½ cups unbleached all-purpose flour

To decorate: Your favorite pre-made vanilla frosting, cookie decorations, and colored sugars

In a large mixing bowl, beat the butter with an electric mixer until soft and fluffy. Add the sugar, baking powder, and salt, and beat until combined. Add the vanilla and egg and beat again, then add the flour and beat for 1 to 2 minutes. Use a wooden spoon to stir in any remaining flour.

Cover and chill the dough for 30 minutes to an hour.

Divide the dough in half and shape each portion into an 8-inch-long roll. Wrap the dough rolls in plastic wrap and chill for at least 4 hours, or up to overnight.

Preheat the oven to 375°F. Cut the cookie dough into ¼-inch-thick slices with a sharp knife and arrange on an ungreased cookie sheet. Sprinkle the cookies with colored sugars, if you like (or top the cookies with icing and decorations after baking). Bake the cookies for 8 to 10 minutes, or until the edges are firm.

INDEX

The Good, the Bad & the Yummy

The Good, the Bad & the Yummy

The Good, the Bad & the Yummy

NOTES

NOTES

NOTES

NOTES